Poverty and Social Exclusion

During and After Poland's Transition to Capitalism

Four Generations of Women in a Post-Industrial City Tell Their Life Stories

WYDAWNICTWO
UNIWERSYTETU
ŁÓDZKIEGO

Paulina Bunio-Mroczek
Małgorzata Potoczna
Wielisława Warzywoda-Kruszyńska

Poverty and Social Exclusion

During and After Poland's Transition to Capitalism

Four Generations of Women in a Post-Industrial City Tell Their Life Stories

JAGIELLONIAN UNIVERSITY PRESS
WYDAWNICTWO UNIWERSYTETU ŁÓDZKIEGO
Łódź–Kraków 2016

Paulina Bunio-Mroczek, Małgorzata Potoczna, Wielisława Warzywoda-Kruszyńska
– University of Łódź, Faculty of Economics and Sociology
Department of Applied Sociology and Social Work, 90-255 Łódź, POW Street no. 3/5
e-mails: paulinabunio@uni.lodz.pl; matmalmar@poczta.onet.pl; zsoul@uni.lodz.pl

The publishing of the book was funded by the Faculty of Economics and Sociology University of Łódź

Published by Łódź University Press & Jagiellonian University Press

First edition, Łódź–Kraków 2016

ISBN 978-83-8088-500-4 – paperback Łódź University Press

ISBN 978-83-23-4274-8 – paperback Jagiellonian University Press

ISBN 978-83-8088-501-1 – electronic version Łódź University Press

ISBN 978-83-23-9630-7 – electronic version Jagiellonian University Press

Łódź University Press
8 Lindleya St., 90-131 Łódź
www.wydawnictwo.uni.lodz.pl
e-mail: ksiegarnia@uni.lodz.pl
phone +48 (42) 665 58 63

WYDAWNICTWO UNIWERSYTETU ŁÓDZKIEGO

Distribution outside Poland
Jagiellonian University Press
9/2 Michałowskiego St., 31-126 Kraków
phone +48 (12) 631 01 97, +48 (12) 663 23 81, fax +48 (12) 663 23 83
cell phone: +48 506 006 674, e-mail: sprzedaz@wuj.pl
Bank: PEKAO SA, IBAN PL 80 1240 4722 1111 0000 4856 3325
www.wuj.pl

JAGIELLONIAN UNIVERSITY PRESS

Contents

Introduction

The overall objective of this book is to provide knowledge about transmission of poverty as a multidimensional phenomenon in the time of Poland's transition to capitalism before the country joined the European Union. There is a huge shortage of publications concerning poverty in the post-socialist period of the Central and Eastern Europe, and we believe that the book will fill the gap. We focus on the experience of women that goes beyond 'feminisation of poverty' traditionally perceived in monetary terms, and search for numerous contributing factors. Therefore the book is also about changes in the social structure, industrial relations, welfare regime and family structures and relations, as well as about the women's capabilities to cope with disadvantages.

It is unique in the sense that it puts subjective experience and efforts of the women suffering from scarcity in the frame of macrostructural processes which are beyond their reach. The book describes family histories of the women who in the previous social system (socialism) belonged to a leading group in the female labour force whereas their daughters, granddaughters, and great-granddaughters need support provided by social assistance, both during and following the system transformation period, since they are unable to earn a living. Therefore the book describes the intra- and inter- generational transmission of poverty as a multidimensional phenomenon documented in family life stories of the women living in disadvantaged urban neighbourhoods and belonging mostly to the same extended families.

As noted by Robert Miller (2007), qualitative research allows to learn about a family's life history and thus better understand the mechanism of the intra- and intergenerational transmission of poverty. Biographical research based on accounts of several family members has, according to him, following advantages:

1. It provides an insight into the subjective construction of meanings by interviewees. *What is crucial is that the analyst can reach an*

understanding of how the interviewee has come to give the responses that he or she does give; both at the surface level of tailoring their responses within the context of the interview and at the more deep level of the actual interpretations of their present and past situations that they have themselves (Miller 2007: 3).
2. It enables the construction of a comprehensive picture of the family, especially when life stories are told by representatives of different generations within the same family.
3. The holistic approach transcends barriers of space and time taking into account events and people previously and presently related to the interviewees.
4. It provides access to information about at least two generations preceding the interviewee, hence one can follow the transfer of resources not only from parents to children but also from grandparents to grandchildren, between siblings, etc.
5. It enables reconstruction of the 'history' of a creation of new households by family members taking into account favourable circumstances and those which impede their formation such as easy or difficult access to housing, work or emotional relations with family members, etc.
6. It reveals differences in perception and assessment of the same events and processes by representatives of different generations from the same family.

We applied in the book the life-course perspective, defined by Giele and Elder (1998) as follows: *The key building block elements of the new life-course paradigm are events combined in event histories or trajectories that are then compared across persons or groups by noting differences in timing, duration, and rates of change. [...] No longer are the principal questions ones of comparing static qualities such as how many and which people are poor; rather, the new dynamic questions focus on both individual characteristics and system properties* (1998: 2).

The above approach is based on five principles (Giele, Elder 1998; Elder, Johnson, Crosnoe 2004; Verd, Lopez 2011; Shanahan, Mortimer, Krikpatrick Johnson 2016) which are addressed in analyses presented in this monograph:

1) time and place – people are embedded in the historical and cultural context affecting their experiences and framing their life-course;
2) linked lives – interactions with other influence actions of individuals and give rise to shared experiences;
3) human agency – people make decisions and act taking into account socio-cultural context;

4) timing – people in different age are affected differently by the same events and therefore their consequences are not the same;
5) life-span development – to understand individual's course of life the long-time perspective has to be applied.

The life-course perspective is mostly applied by quantitatively oriented scholars, but the qualitative studies have increasingly contributed to the approach. In this book we applied a qualitative method (case study), which enabled us to locate actions undertaken by people in the interrelation with external factors even if they did not reflect them (Munck 2004) and in the interrelation with other people.

We followed so-called realistic approach sharing Daniel Bertaux (1997) and Peter Thompson (2004) point of view that the story is a means to access 'objective' reality beyond narrator. Such approach seems to be the most fruitful when individuals are confronted with unexpected and long-lasting challenges leading to destabilisation of the 'usual' life-course

Therefore, in the family life stories one can trace how the main structural factors like industrial relations, family structure and welfare system constituted the frame for decisions taken by the narrators concerning their private and vocational life. Family structures and relations, labour market and welfare system have undergone changes in the analysed time span and differently affected generations under study. They constituted socio-economic-cultural context impacting on decisions and actions of women participating in the research. The oldest generation experienced the quasi-feudal relations before the Second World War, forced labour in German agriculture farms and factories during the WWII, and two system transformations: from capitalism toward socialism and vice versa. Their daughters lived as children and adult persons in the socialist society enjoying secure industrial relations (including extended parental leave available for female workers on their request) and later on had to accommodate to capitalist order. The generation of their granddaughters born mostly in the 1970s attended grammar school still during socialism but grew up under conditions of capitalism and experienced the transformation as mediated by fears and hopes of their parents and when adult as welfare dependency. The youngest generation born during transformation does not know other political and economic order than that produced by neoliberal capitalism.

After the year 1989, the system transformation caused changes in value system establishing the private ownership as fundamental and the most protected one. Market economy replaced command economy, what altogether with reorientation of international economic relations after collapse of the Council of Mutual Economic Assistance covering socialist countries, led to deindustrialization and massive unemployment. The collapse of industrial working class as an influential social segment produced new social divisions. The private possession of means of production, mass media, and a real estate created Haves versus Non-Haves and ability to adjust to new economic requirements (with access to work as an important criterion) generated Winners versus Losers.

Therefore the book contains evidence of the process of de-protelarization, which is reflected in the women's life stories. It shows the loss of self-esteem and personal dignity by the representatives of the working class, which used to be labelled as the 'leading class' in the state socialism. The reader will also observe destandarization of employment, referred to as work flexibility, which led to unpredictability of income and transformation of workers' districts into poverty enclaves.

At the local level, these changes fostered growing economic and social inequalities that translated into spatial segregation. According to Alain Bertaut (2004: 5), development of socialist cities at time of the system transformation was imposed by following circumstances:

1) location of the residential estates of the high-density panel housing on the outskirts,
2) location of industrial land near city centres,
3) lacking space in the city centre for retail and services,
4) poorly maintained infrastructure in the centre with the high residential density,
5) problems with the renovation of houses mostly in the inner-city caused by property rights problems and land tenure.

All above mentioned circumstances operated in the town of Łódź in the 1990s and contributed to the spatial and social segregation forming pockets of poverty (enclaves of poverty) defined as areas where members of households provided with means-tested social assistance benefits constituted at least 30 per cent of population living there. 12 among 17 revealed enclaves of poverty were located in the city centre (Fig.1).

According to Warzywoda-Kruszyńska and Golczyńska-Grondas (2010: 31), three overlapping processes contributed to impoverishment of thousands of Łódź inhabitants in the 1990s, pushing many of them to social and municipal housing in the devastated tenement houses in the city centre:

1. Deindustrialization – closing down of factories led to mass and chronic unemployment.
2. Commodification – increase in rent and commercialization of social services produced arrears and in many causes resulted in eviction.
3. Deinstitutionalization of family – increase in the number of one-person households and single-parent families as well as decrease in the number of marriages contributed to a lower income level.

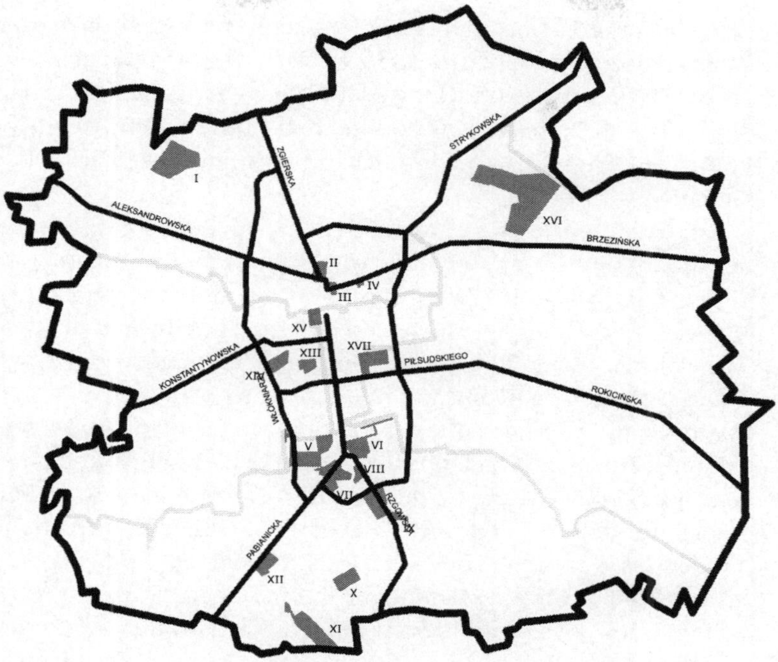

Figure 1. Location of enclaves of poverty in the city of Łódź
Source: Grotowska-Leder J. (1998: 64); the map producer: I. Jażdżewska

The processes were accompanied by severe shortages in the municipal budget and the lack of flats available from the municipal administration, that is the structure responsible for providing low standard shelters to evicted persons[1], and to others, if that was ordered by the court. Two other groups were also eligible for such shelters. They included young adults leaving residential care and foster families, and ex-prisoners without permanent residence.

Apart from the administratively run inflow of low-income individuals and families to the inner-city, where tenement houses were not renovated during the entire post-WWII period and therefore they were in a very bad condition, spontaneous processes also occurred. They included outflow of better-off residents and inflow of those with low income who decided to move into the houses to pay lower rent to avoid eviction. All

1 Pregnant women, families with children, disabled persons and pensioners are protected against eviction 'to nowhere'. Because it is a lack of free social or municipal flats, municipality pays rent to tenant houses owners, what produces huge burden on municipal budget.

these factors contributed to a relatively high concentration of poor people in the centre of the city. The disadvantaged areas that formed at that time still exist. Poverty is a shocking feature characterising these localities. Ten years after the existence of the inner-city poverty pockets in Łódź was confirmed, these places continue to be impoverished neighbourhoods (ibidem p.40).

In the literature, there are different explanations of disadvantage persistence in some locations, emphasising the persistence of unemployment (Kain 1968; Wilson 1987; Johnson 2006) and insecurity resulting from low pay – no pay (Shildrick, McDonald, Webster, Garthwaite 2012), weakness of networks (Buck 2001; Buck, Gordon 2004) and disorder, which discourages better-off people to settle down there. Though all these circumstances applied to Łódź, the explanation by Wacquant (2008) seems to be the most adequate. He claims that neo-liberal capitalism produced *neighbourhoods of relegation* to keep control over individuals excluded from the labour market and forced to exist outside the mainstream of society. In the stories presented in the book there is evidence that people manifest strong feelings of being redundant and relegated.

Living in poverty and social disadvantage produces different consequences depending on age. It is particularly devastating if experienced in childhood (Shonkoff, Philips (eds.) 2000; Shonkoff 2011; Yaqub 2002; Chase-Lansdale, Kiernan, Friedman (eds.) 2004; Lareau 2011; Daly, Leonard 2008; TARKY 2010; de Neubourg, Bradshaw, Chzhen, Main, Martorano, Menchini 2012; Sharkey, Tirado-Strayer, Papachristos, Raver 2012). Poverty in childhood translates frequently into poverty in adulthood and transmits to the subsequent generation. Karen Moore (2004) emphasises that intergenerational transmission of poverty should be studied in close connection with intra-generational poverty/prosperity. She focuses on what is transmitted from parents to children, (external) factors that affect this process and the ways in which they affect it. What is actually transmitted from one generation to another are different types of capital (material, human, environmental, socio-cultural and socio-political). The prosperity of individuals from the next generation depends on whether, and in what form, they received capital from their ancestors and whether they have accrued capital themselves. The transfer of different types of capital and therefore transmission of poverty/prosperity takes place under certain structural and cultural conditions. Some concern the level of family e.g. composition of the household, style of raising children, sex of children, while others operate at the level of local community and neighbourhood e.g. accessibility of social services or at a macro level i.e. at the level of society e.g. legal norms which regulate inheritance rules and access to capital.

However, transmission of poverty across generations is not a deterministic process. Individual's agency, frequently referred to as resistance, and external intervention may change such course of life. We can observe it in the life stories of the oldest generation. On the other hand, better-off childhood may transfer into scarcity in adulthood, as documented in the life histories of younger generation. Poverty drivers include unemployment of the parents, family disruption, moving in the pocket of poverty and meeting peers and adults who disrespect social norms and behaviours, etc.

The specific objectives of the book to realize by means of analysing family life histories of women belonging to four subsequent generations was getting better understanding of:

1) formative biographical events impacting women's entrenchment in poverty, its persistence and possible overcoming,
2) biographical experiences formative for each generation of women,
3) typical ways of experiencing biographical events by women from each generation,
4) socio-economic and historical processes underlying the course of subjective women's experiences,
5) patterns of experiencing poverty identified in all generations,
6) drivers and maintainers of poverty transmission across generations.

To achieve these objectives we considered empirical data from two studies carried out by a team of sociologists working for the University of Łódź:

1. 'Forms of Poverty and Social Threats and their Spatial Distribution in Łódź'[2] (1996–1999), and
2. 'Teenage parenthood as exposure to poverty and social exclusion' – the module in the research project 'WZLOT – Strengthening Opportunities and Weakening the Intergenerational Transmission of Poverty among Inhabitants of Łódź Voivodeship'[3] (2008–2010).

---

2 PBZ nr 018 08 was financed by the Scientific Research Committee (KBN). Results of the project were published in a series of books and articles, for example Warzywoda-Kruszyńska W. (eds.) (1998) *Żyć i pracować w enklawach biedy*. Łódź; Warzywoda-Kruszyńska W. (eds.) (1999) *(Żyć) Na marginesie wielkiego miasta*. Łódź; Golczyńska-Grondas A. (2004) *Mężczyźni z enklaw biedy: rekonstrukcja pełnionych ról społecznych*. Łódź; Potoczna M., Warzywoda-Kruszyńska W. (2009) *Kobiety z łódzkich enklaw biedy. Bieda w cyklu życia i międzypokoleniowym przekazie*. Łódź. Wydawnictwo UŁ.

3 UDA-POKL.07.02.01-10-033/08-00). Results of the project are available at: www.wzlot.uni.lodz.pl.

Both studies are based on the family life history method as developed in P. Thompson's oral history tradition. Each respondent was asked to tell her/his family history. A few interviews are narrative, and they were collected among the women from the oldest generation. In cases where it was not possible to conduct purely narrative interviews, in-depth interviews were performed. All these interviews were recorded and transcribed *in extenso* covering almost 2000 pages of transcription.

To obtain empirical data with the purpose not only to describe life-courses of different generations but also to explain the inter-generational transmission of poverty and social disadvantage, the study conducted in 1998 included adult members of the extended families, belonging to at least two generations. We decided to limit the research to females more or less embedded in the extended families to get a better insight into family relations that may function as both the cause of poverty and social deprivation and protection against this phenomenon. The core group of respondents was composed of social welfare recipients[4], aged between 45–50 years, living in the inner-city enclaves of poverty.

Selection of the narrators was the multi-stage process:

1. Social workers acting in the enclaves of poverty selected female welfare recipients aged between 45–50 years.
2. They gave them preliminary information about the research project and asked them whether they would be ready to participate in the research.
3. Among those who wished to participate, social workers selected those who declared having some family relations with ascendants (mother, father, grandmother, or grandfather) or adult descendants (daughter, son, granddaughter, or grandson), preferably having a separate household.
4. After receiving the informed consent by a given social welfare recipient and at least one of her ascendants or descendants, the research team approached them.

Due to such selection criteria the population to participate in the project was limited. Unfortunately, many of the selected potential participants withdrew from the research. There were different reasons for that decision, such as shortage of time, deteriorating family relations, illness, incarceration, etc. There were also situations where despite having accepted the researcher's visit, potential narrators were unavailable without giving any excuse. One of the explanations of such behaviour might be the sense of shame caused by substandard housing conditions of the po-

4 Social assistance is provided on means-tested basis for people with no or very low income.

tential respondents. The potential respondents were asked to accept the interviewers in their flats since the researchers wanted to observe their living conditions to report them in the materials. Many respondents lived in flats in devastated tenement houses, which made some of them feel uncomfortable.

We have collected 90 biographical interviews in total, and they covered 40 extended families. 10 families included representatives of three generations, while the remaining 30 families included representatives of two. The whole group of respondents included 56 women, and the interviews with them provided the basis for this publication: 15 women belonged to the oldest generation (referred to as 'grandmothers'), 25 to the middle generation (referred to as 'mothers') and 16 to the younger generation (referred to as 'daughters'). Seven families were represented by three generations of women, and ten families by two. In 15 families a son or a father acted as the second interviewee.

We focused on the women's experiences since we assume that poverty and mechanisms of its perpetuation are gender related[5]. We also assume that poor people living in the pockets of poverty are most exposed to intra- and inter-generational transmission of poverty and social deprivation, as a result of *neighbourhood effects*. William Julius Wilson (1987) described them as spatial segregation and social isolation. They affect opportunities of the inhabitants, chaining them to one place and limiting their possibilities of economic and social mobility. Loïc Wacquant (2007) referred to such places as *neighbourhoods of relegation* to underline structural causes of the creation of such localities.

However, results presented in the book do not concern all poverty enclaves inhabitants or even all women living there. In 1998, we focused on women who were not severely socially isolated. They kept in touch with close relatives not only to the extent that they could recommend and motivate them to take part in the research but also offering each other informal support. Belonging to the same extended family, they provided us with information on facts (sometimes hidden by another representative of their family) which enabled to reconstruct and better understand processes and social mechanisms contributing to the poverty transmission. In the stories provided by women belonging to each generation there were facts and events revealed by representatives of the subsequent generation. For example 'grandmothers' were not talking at all about violence

5 On a basis of interviews with men collected within the project Agnieszka Golczyńska-Grondas published in 2004 the book *Mężczyźni z enklaw biedy: rekonstrukcja pełnionych ról społecznych*.

they and their children experienced. The 'mothers' hid the fact that they were pregnant before marriage or that their children from first marriage often grew up in grandmothers households. Therefore, family life histories reported by adult representatives of different generations of the same extended family are of a particular importance.

The events reported in this research project did not go beyond 1998. Therefore, to include the experiences of the next generation of women living in the enclaves of poverty we took the opportunity that arose from the research module 'Teenage parenthood as exposure to poverty and social exclusion' in the project 'WZLOT – Strengthening Opportunities and Weakening the Intergenerational Transmission of Poverty among Inhabitants of Łódź Voivodeship'. The primary intention of the project was to get a better understanding of how early parenthood in the enclave of poverty contributed to staying poor as adults. However, it occurred that the group of female respondents included the women who belonged to the generation whose members were minors in 1998, when the first research project was carried out. Therefore, including their experience enabled us to broaden the life-course analysis including an additional generation of women whose entire life experience occurred after the fall of socialist order.

The research covered women and men, although in this book we are only concerned with female respondents. They had to meet following criteria:

1) to bear a child as a teenager (up to 20 years of age),
2) to live in an enclave of poverty,
3) to be a member of a household provided with means-tested social assistance benefit and/or child allowance provided for low-income families on a basis of means-test,
4) to be in their twenties.

Due to the above criteria, selection of the respondents was a challenging issue. First of all, we tried to select them from the list of social welfare recipients and child allowance recipients, which was provided by public administration institutions. Unfortunately, this method turned to be ineffective. Therefore, we asked social workers serving in the enclaves of poverty to contact us with persons meeting the criteria, if they work with some. When the first few potential respondents were selected, we applied a snowball procedure to contact other respondents. Altogether 73 women participated in the project. Keeping their parental rights is a characteristic that distinguishes them. It means that social services accepted the ways in which they took care of their children. We know from our previous studies that mothers living in enclaves of poverty are often deprived of parental rights. Numerous refusals to participate in the project made us assume that they might be those teenage mothers whose children were in foster care.

In the group of 73 interviewees, only 11 were born in 1989 and 1990 and their experience provides the foundation for presenting life histories of the youngest generation, referred to as 'granddaughters'. They resemble respondents approached under the first study based on the fact that they have at least on child, although are not related to women who were interviewed ten years earlier. However, one will notice that their life experience resembles very much the experience told by other young women in the study group.

Due to the sample selection specifics, readers are asked to remember that the book is only about poor women living in disadvantaged urban neighbourhoods, who struggled to fulfil their parental obligations. It does not mean that in the extended families, which are the subject of this book, all adults cared for their children.

The book is structured as follows: it begins with a chapter summarising the sociological approach to the life–course based on biographical material. The next four chapters present results concerning: the oldest generation ('grandmothers'), the middle generation ('mothers'), the young generation ('daughters') and the youngest generation ('granddaughters'). Then sociological portraits of three extended families are presented. Conclusions constitute the last paragraph of the book.

Chapter 1
The sociology of the life course

The issue of human life is the subject of biographical research from a sociological perspective. This research includes all studies in which the subject is the biography of an individual, group or institution, regardless of the study's adopted methodological orientation. Theoretical concepts of researchers who represent the interpretive approach play a special role in the reconstruction of biographical experiences. These concepts include the concept of process structures by Fritz Schütze (Schütze 1981, 1983) the concept of identity and trajectory by Anselm Strauss (Glaser, Strauss 1968 1970, Strauss 1987) and the concept of moral career by Erving Goffman (Goffman 1978, 1979) among others. This approach is also favoured by Norman Denzin, whose concept of epiphany – key biographical events – underlines that important events, turning points or epiphanies are identifiable in the life of every individual: *[epiphanies] which constitute a type of biographical axis and basic structure of meaning around which an individual organises other types of his/her life activities and which often change his/her life course* (Denzin 1989).

In the seventies, the theoretical model of life-course analysis was suggested as part of the emerging sub-discipline of biographical research – the sociology of the life course. This model takes into account new, biographical aspects of the interrelation between the individual and society which have emerged as a consequence of social changes in such areas of activity as professional work, family life or leisure time (Hajduk 2001). The notion of biography, predominantly in line with the understanding proposed as part of the biographical method, has remained the key notion in the sociology of the life course. The perspective under discussion perceives the individual's life course both in terms of categories of consecutive major biographical events encountered by an individual in the course of his/her life which determine subsequent stages of his/her life comprising the biographical structure of the life course (childhood, adolescence, youth, adulthood, old age) to a large extent (Marshall 2004), and in terms of *the dynamic qualitative process of changes which occur in the period from childhood to death in different dimensions of his/her life activity based on biological and socio-cultural criteria under the influence of these events* (Neugarten, Hagestad 1976: 36). This concept emphasises that the consecutive stages which define the biographical structure of the life course should be seen from the perspective of their interrelatedness although they are not always intended or planned. Throughout the course of their linear biography, individuals may find themselves in situations similar to those they have previously experienced. *The life course is a sequence of events which constitutes a partially intended and partially unintended process, in which earlier events determine subsequent events* (Harris 1987: 21–22). According to Danuta Dobrowolska, *the life course is a sequence of human experiences and behaviours (including actions) related to specific situations that an individual encounters from the moment of birth until death which are determined both by the transformation of the body and psyche of a given individual and by changing external conditions in a broad sense* (Dobrowolska 1992: 77). The individual's life course is seen as an integral part of social life. *Social reality also has a biographical dimension. Social phenomena and processes leave an imprint on life course models, elicit competence typically biographical in nature* (Prawda 1989: 82).

Researchers who apply this research perspective share the following subjects of their interest:

1) social construction (patterns) of the life course, namely its institutional structuration as defined by norms and requirements of social institutions,
2) implementation of social constructions, namely the life course understood as the realisation of possibilities of attaining individual biographical aspirations in different areas of activity determined by socially defined standards and conditions outlining the possibilities of achieving this pattern,
3) complex relations between both components of social reality.

An analysis of 'the social construction of the life course' focuses on patterns of the life course, that is standards of an individual's participation in various areas of activity, socio-cultural and institutional conditions typical of a given society which determine the prospects of attaining biographical aspirations. Cultural patterns of the life course fulfil two key functions: first of all, they constitute a social orientation pattern for an individual which outlines his/her opportunities to fulfil biographical aspirations/ambitions as well as the desirable, acceptable and admissible life course as measured by legal, moral and customary norms. This motivates an individual, enables life planning, unleashes his/her activity. Secondly, cultural patterns of the life course cement the continuity of culture and social repeatability of individual life courses. They therefore constitute the normative component of culture and the institutional organisation of society of a given historical formation. They reflect perspectives of realisations of biographical aspirations of individuals created by society (Hajduk 2001). Research into patterns of the life course is therefore an *identification of chances of realisation of individual biographical aspirations in a given historical period, of possible personal patterns, patterns of individual biography, defined by socially determined choices and standards used to measure success* (Hajduk 2001: 46). The possibility of realising biographical aspirations, that is real, actual patterns of the life course, vary according to age, sex, profession or affiliation with social groups as well as strong conditioning by the organisation and the institutional order of a society. The system of existing institutions individuals belong to and their functional diversity create conditions which are fundamental to shaping acquired biographical patterns. Institutionalisation imposes an objectified, cultural scheme of development which determines individual requirements (Hajduk 2001).

The life course understood as 'social construction' structures the succession of the various social roles played by an individual during their life as well as their participation in institutions which define the way these roles are fulfilled. Social roles define different types of activity. Areas of activity and fulfilled roles constitute cultural bases for adopted life decisions. *Societies have complex systems of social roles which define possible choices within an individual's life course* (Hajduk 2001: 49).

When 'the realisation of social construction' of the life course understood as the reconstruction of individual ways of 'making biography real' by the selected category of individuals becomes the subject of the analysis, *the life course means an individual's adherence to the standards of the organisation of society and its structural diversification* (Hajduk 2001: 48). In this context, the life course is defined as 'individual making-real (realisation) of the social pattern of the life course' – a personal interpretation of that which an individual should achieve with respect to different areas of his or her activity. Making biography real therefore reveals subjective, sequential and temporal aspects of the individual's life course. It informs about the experience and activity of a given individual. It treats his/her life course as a process *which defines a sequence of different events and biographical situations as well as individual actions which may (may not) correspond to a scenario typical of a given pattern in a given social timeframe* (Hajduk 2001: 57). In this sense, the life course reflects a unique means of realising values which constitute the axiological fundamentals of the organisation of society as well as the way in which the individual participates in social institutions. The social pattern of the individual life course, as made real, comprises both structure and experience as well as action as the research subject. The life course understood as 'making biography real' therefore structures *a sequence of subsequent events, experiences and actions which are assigned different meanings and which constitute a component of the general culture of society* (Hajduk 2001: 50).

When the subject of the analysis of the life course comprises relations between both components of biographical reality, attention is paid to the unique means by which biography is made real under certain historical circumstances, to the relationship between the institutionalisation of the life course and the desire to manage one's own life independently and to make one's own life choices.

Individual life experience acquired by an individual during his/her lifetime constitutes the key factor in his/her development. It is determined by that which an individual encounters in terms of experienced events, situations and own actions (Przetacznik-Gierowska, Tyszkowa 1996). The following experiences combine to make up the cumulative individual biographical experience:

1) experiences of the species, transmitted by inheritance,
2) individual experiences gained during the course of one's own activity and events in different spheres of life,
3) social experiences gained during the course of communication processes with others, culture acquisition through socialisation and upbringing (Przetacznik-Gierowska, Tyszkowa 1996).

Biographical events are attributed an essential role in the construction of life experience. *An event in the life of every individual constitutes an important change in his/her situation (entirely or with regards to some of its elements) that occur in a relatively short time frame, at least partially independently of his/her will* (Dobrowolska 1992: 82). Biographical events in the human life course fulfil two basic functions:

1) they structure and determine the direction of the individual's life course as solid, biographical facts,
2) they transform and modify the life course and determine qualitative changes in the life of an individual as processes.

In the concept of the life course under discussion, special attention is paid to interrelations between the life event and the scope and type of changes it triggers. Each event is treated as a biographical fact which can be attributed to a greater or lesser significant impact on an individual's subsequent fate, since each one – due to the modification potential it entails – can change the existing way of living, sometimes in an insignificant way and sometimes decisively. Depending on the type of changes induced, opportunities for development may appear or disappear, they may constitute a source of new experiences, prompt changes in the psyche, change the individual's status, lead to a lack of continuity of biography, change aspirations and life goals. Changes can be either functional or dysfunctional, critical or trajectory-like. They can be conservative (reproducing the dominant structural system) or evolutionary (create a new structural system) in their nature (Hoerning 1990). Each event requires an adaptive effort on behalf of an individual. It forces one to undertake actions and to elect a given strategy (the abandonment of activity is also an action) designed to change the life situation. Some actions may entail devising constructive solutions to difficult problems. Other actions result in a loss of control over an individual's life and an unidentified position (life trajectory, in F. Schütze's terms). The scope and nature of changes that a given event introduces as well as the ways of coping with the event, that is behaviours and strategies for coping with the event, define the ways in which it is experienced. The ways in which life events are experienced are largely determined according to:

1) the individual's biographical resources defined by the capital attributed to him/her or acquired by him/her which may take the form of material, social, cultural and educational possibilities as well as existing experience acquired through the encountering of earlier events (given that these experiences are updated or revived), depend on the age, degree of sensitivity, ability to reflect as well as adopted values,
2) socio-structural resources which provide one with socially acceptable patterns, that is possibilities of solving life problems – social interpretive patterns – socially acceptable ways of problem-solving (Hoerning 1990).

While explaining fates based on life events, it is important to identify socio-cultural opportunities accessible to an individual at a given moment in history as well as the lived life experiences which led to the formulation of his/her current biographical perspective (Hoerning 1990).

Literature concerning the subject proposes various classifications of life events[1]. The typology of events proposed by E. H. Hoerning covers three categories of events which can be described as formative, that is they determine the material status of an individual, his/her social status, relations with other people and they impact fates both in terms of individual and collective dimensions of biography.

1 Psychological literature lists the probability of event occurrence, correlation with age and the number of people as well as the impact of stress as basic criteria of the classification of life events (Przetacznik-Gierowska, Tyszkowa 1996).

These events are as follows:

1) normative events which constitute a boundary between different phases of life (events related to the life cycle),
2) random events, and
3) historical events.

The first category includes experiences (common for most people) related to the passage of individuals to the subsequent age categories which constitute the boundary between different stages of life. These are primarily: the beginning and the end of schooling, undertaking employment, marriage, birth of children, end of occupational activity, retirement. Each of the stages can, to a greater or lesser extent, be consciously planned or elicited by the decisions of a given individual subject to the existence of different preconditions.

The next group constitutes random events, correlated with age to a lesser extent, experienced by a smaller number of people. At different life stages, they emerge suddenly and unexpectedly. As a result, an individual finds himself/herself in an entirely different situation or in a situation which radically changes his/her life path. These events include: an accident with long-term consequences; sudden illness; death of a loved one; job loss or forced change of job; commission of criminal act; dissolution of marriage or an accident.

The third category outlined includes historical events resulting from macro-structural processes which affect society at large and create a framework for individual actions. Primarily, they include wars, socio-economic system changes, economic crises and mass unemployment. They often take the form of generational events which unite people of similar ages. Involvement in overall political, cultural and economic conditions brings about similar ways of thinking, behaviours, worldviews and assessments of one's own social situation in the process of social socialisation which constitute decisive factors in terms of belonging to a given generation. Historical processes shape collective biographies and have a clearly identifiable impact on succession of periods and phases of individual's biographies (Hoering 1990). As stated by Daniel Bertaux (1995: 12), *Macro-social processes are reflected in family lives. There are processes which lead individuals and entire families from situations of relative stability to situations of poverty.* The scope and resources of individual biographical experience are diversified in line with socio-historical context. Diverse historical conditions define the diversity of forms of life activity and the similarity of experiences and fates of individuals of the same generation. *General social and economic situations, changes that occur within them and various types of political events explain many objective facts relating to an individual's life as well as his/her experiences and social identity. The fact of belonging to the same generation affects the similarity of courses of lives and relations with persons of other generations* (Dobrowolska 1992: 78). Events which can be categorised as groundbreaking events (turning points) play a special role in an individual's biographical experience. Any experienced life event can become a turning point. Subjective feelings of a given individual determine whether a given event comes to acquire the status of a turning point. *These are the events which are perceived as having a major impact on an individual, changing their life course, dramatically transforming their social environment, changing their psyche and identity* (Dobrowolska 1992: 84). Turning points usually occur when there is an accumulation of several important life events. Arising as a result of historical events, they are associated with significant psychological experiences, changes of identity and worldviews.

Biographical research has many adherents in sociology who point to both highly theoretical and practical values of biographical data as *a source of well-grounded knowledge and ideal material for sociological research* (Thomas, Znaniecki 1958 after: Kohli 1981: 63), *which enables the exploration and understanding of the depth of the functioning of an individual, group and society as well as the verification of theoretical assumptions* (Rzepa, Leoński 1993: 7). According to Daniel Bertaux, the *biographical approach gives one direct access to the level of social relations which comprise the very essence of sociological knowledge, since most of the biographical materials (regardless of the means by which they are collected) conserve the nature of personal accounts of one's own life history* (Bertaux 1981: 31)[2]. There are several reasons which determine the high cognitive value of biographical research. This research:

1) allows familiarisation with social reality through informal means by referring directly to everyday, diverse, interrelated personal experiences and the emotions of the individual. By getting to know them, one can not only explain but also, and above all, understand what people feel and think, what their motives are when they undertake actions, what meaning is ascribed to individual situations and events, what experiences are prompted by certain social and cultural conditions in a given reality. The meaning that biographies contain is both biographical and historical in nature. Lived experience is an emotional and cognitive process (Rzepa, Leoński 1993). Biography *represents experiences and definitions by a given person, group or organisation in the way this person, group*

2 Biographical documents comprise life histories, biographies, life stories, case stories, case studies, autobiographies, letters, diaries, personal documents and narrative interviews (Leoński 1993).

or organisation interprets these experiences. The overall goal of biographical analysis is to discover the meaning behind the experiences of ordinary people (Denzin 1990: 55);

2) allows the discovery, explanation and understanding of typical forms and patterns of human thinking, behaviours, perceptions and assessments of historical phenomena, rules of entering social relations, determinants of fulfilment of social roles, typical biographical moments, means of reaching understanding and clarifying a situation, undertaking actions, coming to terms with everyday reality, and above all, understanding of the meanings attributed to events, processes and life structures by placing emphasis on the *lived experiences* of individuals;
3) provides a holistic view of social reality, its order, logic, covert and overt principles *from within*, that is in semantic categories attributed by the subjective individual;
4) reveals processes of social becoming of a subject, that is *constant integration between the awareness of the individual and objective social reality* (Thomas, Znaniecki 1958) (after: Kohli 1981: 62);
5) biography presented by the individual is not merely a reflection of the individual on their experiences, it presents the process of structuring of the image of oneself and the development of one's self (Hankiss 1981);
6) allows the capturing of social life in its historical dimension (Kohli 1981)[3].

3 Few researchers undermine the cognitive value of such research. They rely on the argument that these data lose objectivity, representativeness and comparability and hence, their scientific status due to their retrospective and highly introspective nature. The content of this research is, on the one hand, rendered relative depending on the individual under study and, on the other, is to a large extent, dependent on the theoretical interpretation of the researcher (Leoński 1993; Cichocki 1993).

Chapter 2

Poverty in the biographical experience of women from the oldest generation – 'grandmothers'[1]

The lifetime of the 'grandmother' generation is marked by significant historical events, including the war, the introduction of socialism and intensive industrialisation, as well as the later liquidation of socialism and restitution of capitalism. Although their active involvement in creating their biographies was huge, for these women it was also undoubtedly conditioned by external circumstances. Their paths through life were determined by pre-war poverty, experience obtained during the German occupation, as workers in socialist factories, and at the end of their lives (in many cases) as sole providers for their extended families. Beginning in poverty, in childhood, their lives have led them through periods of low-level stability in adulthood, back to poverty at the end of their lifetimes. For the 'grandmother' generation, the chain of poverty was interrupted as a result of external circumstances – the introduction of socialism and industrialisation. They took the chance to escape from poverty, which had been created by post-war industrialisation and the intensified vocational activation of women. From being beggars in the villages where they lived before the WWII, they became respected workers whose day was divided into working and leisure time, and who took leave and had holidays, as well as nurseries and summer camps for their children, pro-

1 The oldest generation – 'grandmothers' (the mothers of the key respondents) – are represented by females aged 65 to 85. Two were married, while the other respondents were widows for several years. Two of them run one-person households, while the others run households together with their grownup children or grandchildren, for whom they constituted foster family. Their low retirement pensions were the main source of the means of maintenance. All the respondents assessed their financial status as bad, for the following reasons: low old-age pension, having to support their unemployed grownup children and grandchildren (some of whom abuse alcohol), having to care for their grownup, seriously ill children, and having to provide foster care for their grandchildren when the parents have failed to care for them properly.

vided by factories they worked for. But after system transformation, these women's living conditions are hard, and this is not only due to low old-age pensions, but first of all because of the unemployment of their grown up children and grandchildren, whom they need to support financially. When they were young, they were often the sole providers or co-providers for their parents and younger siblings, and now they are again, for their ascendants. Biographies of this generation of women include facts, situations, and circumstances that force them to shoulder the responsibility of others. This is a generation whose life can be described as *living for others* – where 'living' means 'giving'.

Poverty and the Nazi-German occupation of Poland (1939-1945) were significant facts during these women's childhood and adolescence. The events and their consequent experience resulted in their individual biographies including an unconditional readiness to work hard. During their forced labour for the German farmers, the women became familiar with different techniques and different ways of living. They became open-minded and ready to make changes in their personal life. Having come back to Poland when the World War II was over, they left behind underdeveloped villages, inhabited by multi-child families, characterised by backwardness and incapacity. They took on the risk of an independent life and the search for work in the big cities.

Adulthood was a successful period in their lives, and they recall this period sentimentally, particularly when they compare it to the lives of their children, who at the age of forty-or fifty years are repeating the history of their grandparents from the pre-war period, suffering from unemployment and poverty. The respondents avoided such fate. In their generation, adulthood was marked by the taking up of jobs and starting of families. They were pioneers in the field of the paid employment of women, and their work resulted in relative economic independence and security in their old age. The 'grandmothers' were the vanguard of the emerging big-city working class, which during the time of the Polish People's Republic was referred to as the leading social force. Nevertheless, they implemented a traditional biographical pattern, suspended between the old values and standards, and the new possibilities offered by the socialist social and political system. Jobs, marriage and children marked critical points in their lives. They usually worked for one state owned factory and lived with their husbands until their death. Relatives caused problems that they had to resolve, particularly drunkenness and the irresponsibility of their spouses. And they tried to hide this information from others, including the interviewer – even when the husband had failed to meet expectations. Although divorces became legal in Poland shortly after the WW II and they were able to exercise this right, they hardly ever dissolved the marriage through divorce. However, their self-confidence was high, which resulted from their relative economic independence. They continued to be wives 'until death do us part', even though their families lost their traditional and patriarchal nature. The women were able to distance themselves from their husbands and ensure that the children were provided for, mainly due to their extremely hard work. Not all of the respondents reconciled work and family effectively and were able to be successful in both spheres. At the end of their lives, they had to pay a high cost, from the fact that they not always managed to raise their children to become responsible employees and parents. However, a certain dose of 'modernity' is visible in a clearly smaller number of their children. These poorly educated women from very low-income multi-child families did not continue the family-size pattern of their families of origin. Most of them stopped procreating after giving birth to a second child. Women having had a greater number of children are very rare. Finally, their old age overlapped with the socio-economic system transformation of Poland, the beginnings of their disability, becoming old-age pensionist, the death of their spouses, and the need to support their children and grandchildren through the 'gift of accommodation', and the 'gift of time' (Szukalski 2003). The risk of poverty returned, accompanied by fear for the future of their grandchildren and great-grandchildren. The 'grandmothers' turned out to be the only extended family members having regular income in the form of mothly paid old-age pension allowance.

1. Childhood

1.1. Poverty in childhood in the countryside

The childhoods of the women of the 'grandmother' generation were marked by poverty. Only one respondent had relatively good living conditions, and another experienced a significant improvement, when *de facto* she was illegally adopted.

Poverty was a consequence of structural conditions[2] (economic underdevelopment and structural unemployment in rural areas), local civ-

---

2 The interwar period in rural areas was characterised by the intensifying phenomenon of *agrarian poverty* (which began in the mid-19th century). This was caused by an increase in the number of small and micro farms, itself a result of the Enfranchisement Reform of 1864. The unfavourable structure of agricultural property in rural areas was intensified by a crisis in agriculture (1873–1895), which resulted in

ilisation's backwardness (no skills to control fertility and the resulting multi-children families), and the poor provision and functioning of the social protection system. The natural social security system, which was based on family and the nearest neighbours, dominated in rural areas. However, families were often reconstructed following the death of their founders. A large number of the respondents' siblings are partly the result of the fact that their mother or father remarried – even several times – other widowers with their own offspring from previous marriages, and then had further children with them. *There were quite a few of us, dad was a widower, his first wife died and mum married a widower who had eight children, and later mum had seven, there were the eight children and seven of us, so altogether there were 15 of us (Q/3); I do not remember my mum, I was 15 months old when she died, she was 31 years old, father did not wait for too long, as there were many small children, and he had to get married (F/3). There were children of three mothers, but the mother, although she was a stepmother, she was very reliable, she treated everyone in the same way, no one got something better or worse, everyone received the same portion of food, she poured a meal into a big bowl, and we all set around the table and had enough to eat* (F/3).[3]

The fact that families had to raise many children in conditions of very scarce resources had an obvious impact on the living standard of the respondents' families of origin. However, their order of birth and whether they were a child of the current mother or father were also significant. The elder children's biological parents were in most cases deceased, and in a way it was natural for them to have to earn a living working as 'serv-

---

a decrease in cereal prices that slowed down the process of mechanisation of agriculture, as well as a slowing down in the intensification of agricultural production. As a result of property fragmentation caused by division of inheritance, as well as due to a high birth rate (a demographic explosion in the late 19th and early 20th century), the problem of excessive numbers of workers intensified, which led to the phenomenon of so-called *agrarian overpopulation*. Between 1904 and 1921, the share of micro farms with an area from 1.5 ha to 2 ha rose from 15.1% to 34%, while the share of farms with areas from 2 to 5 ha fell from 46.5% to 30.7%. After a period of relative stability in the 1920s, the financial status of the rural population deteriorated again in the Great Depression of 1929–1935. Moreover, opportunities to migrate from the country became scarcer in comparison to the situation prior to 1918 (with the economic crisis in industry and America's tightening of migration regulations, which limited the inflow of immigrants) (Smykowski 2002).

3 Interviewees' statements presented in chapters 2, 3, 4 and 6 were also used in the book *Kobiety z łódzkich enklaw biedy. Bieda w cyklu życia i międzypokoleniowym przekazie (Women from Łódź Poverty Enclaves. Poverty in the Life Course and Intergenerational Transmssion)* by Małgorzata Potoczna, Wielisława Warzywoda-Kruszyńska (2009), Łódź: University Press.

ants' for other families (See Section 1.1.1). The same was true of those who had lost both parents, even if they remained a 'formal' member of their step-family. In very poor families children had to work as servants, even though both their parents were alive, which indicates that the children were very young.

Financial difficulties were not only due to the small size of the farmland, but also to the poor quality of the soil. *We had 15 morgens, but there were 16 children. So you had to feed the children, and the soil was mainly sand, so the potatoes that grew in that sand had the size of small nuts* (F/3).

This is how the respondents described their childhood: *We were so poor that there was no money to buy salt* (DX/3). *Before the war, there was nothing but work and poverty, nothing else* (I/3). Another respondent reports: *I was poorly dressed, I had one dress for holidays, and the other for work. If I washed the festive one, I was wearing the other one. I had canvas sneakers and clogs, and I had shoes, which I was allowed to wear only to church. In wintertime I was wearing knee-high boots, because I had knee-high boots, and in summertime I was walking barefoot* (B/3). Everything needed to survive was homemade. In some families, the mothers were spinning flax and made clothes for all the family, since there was no money to purchase fabric. *Mum used to spin flax, and made shirts for us from it, because such shirts were not available in those days. She used canvas to make shirts, or maybe a blouse made of canvas she had made herself, and then she dyed the blouse* (F/3). *Mother used to make the clothes herself as she could not afford to buy them, so she never spent money on clothes* (O/3). Daily-use footwear was also made at home. *My brother knew how to make shoes, he carved the outsoles in wood, then removed* [the top part] *from normal shoes, fixed it to the wooden part, and we wore such shoes to school, to slide on ice, he was very creative. The shoes he made were so nice, and we were happy* (F/3). Normal shoes were worn only to church. Household equipment was also homemade.

Families lived in small two-room houses made of timber or clay. *It occupied about 22 metres, before the war we did not even have a kitchen, there was a small shed, and a tiled stove, baking, cooking, sleeping, everything in one place* (I/3). The grandparents, who transferred the farm to the parents, usually also, lived in the house. *There were five of us* [children], *and it was hard, because there were so many children, and also the grandparents* (I/3). Where there was only one room, everyone slept in the same room. Where there were two rooms, one was occupied by the grandparents. *Three of us slept there, bed by bed, there was no electricity, and we only had an oil lamp* (Q/3). *We often slept in the grandparents' room, two slept in one bed* (I/3). *Two or three slept in one bed, there were four beds in the big room. When the boys were bigger, they all went to work as servants, and then there were fewer of us, and the sleeping arrangements changed* (F/3).

Childhood poverty in the biographical experience of these women of the oldest generation is associated with hunger. They often experienced hunger in their lifetime. *Sometimes I only had a potato with salt to eat* (Q/3). *We had dry bread with milk and potatoes, mum cooked borscht and cabbage* (B/3). Sometimes vegetables or potatoes grown by the parents were not enough to meet the nutritional needs of a large family, so they also bred animals – sometimes they had a horse, a cow, hens, or a pig. The mothers baked bread, and cooked simple meals on a daily basis. *Before the war, we usually had white borscht, almost every day, and potatoes for breakfast. I hated the borscht. For lunch we had dumplings, pierogi* [a kind of tortellini] *which were often made of cottage cheese, soup, and for dinner we got bread and butter, with something to make it a sandwich* (I/3). *Mum cooked everything that could be cooked – peas, beans, barley soup, mum used to dry apples and pears – she even cooked soup from dried* [fruit], *and cabbage which was pickled. Sauerkraut soup was cooked, and potatoes were stored in clamps* (Q/3). There were also situations where potatoes and cabbage were the main food available to families. *Mother softened some rye in steam, and ground it in a grinder and then mixed it with potatoes* (DX/3). Meat was hardly ever served. Sunday meals did not differ much from the meals served on ordinary days. Only some families could afford a two-course Sunday lunch. *We had chicken soup or another soup, and then meat was served for the second course* (I/3). *Mum always bought something to eat for Sunday. Black pudding or a piece of sausage, or she killed a hen, or we had something made of meat* (F/3). Meat was also sometimes served for lunch during the season of intensive field labour. Most families had meat only on holidays: *Mum slaughtered poultry only for holidays* (B/3). *For holidays she baked a sweet bread loaf, and we got a piece of sausage; sometimes, if they bred a pig and slaughtered it, they made some sausage* (Q/3).

1.1.1. Children working as servants

In the experience of the 'grandmothers' generation poverty is associated with work as a servant. This usually meant starting work in early childhood for wealthier farmers, or in rarer cases, in cities. Maintaining all of the family members on a small farm was a serious problem. Parents had to work hard to satisfy all needs.

Most of the field labour was done manually, and they did not only work on their own farms. Financial shortages forced them to search for additional sources of income. Usually, the fathers had to earn additional means to maintain their families, which is why they often worked for wealthier farmers. The mothers ran the household, worked on the farm, and raised the children. Today's 'grandmothers' remember that their mothers spent all their time working on the farm. They had to perform most duties at home and on the farm. *Mum was always busy, she had to cook lunch, milk cows three times a day, feed the pigs, she had to do all chores, and had no time to sit down, however she often prayed with a Rosary, and even when she was walking, she managed to pray* (I/3). The fathers' extra work was not sufficient to maintain families with many children, thus the mothers also had to work for wealthier farmers during summer and autumn harvests. Children were involved in field work on the parents' farms at a young age. *Everyone worked in the field* (I/3); *Everyone did what they could. When my parents were working in the field, I had to deliver lunch for them, although I was a little girl then* (Q/3). In most cases the respondents had to terminate their education to work as servants, to earn their living and help support their families. *I only completed two years at school and then started working for a farmer as a cattle minder, I was 10, or maybe 11 years old, he paid me a few groszy (pence)* (B/3); *I was the eldest child in our family and had to work very hard, I had to mind the cattle, I worked as a servant, my life was hard, very hard* (B/3); *I was 14 years old when I left home to work as a servant* (F/3). For the earnings they received for minding cattle, fieldwork, or doing other chores 'at the farmers', they could only buy a sack of potatoes, or a little flour. Gratification for their servant's work also included food, agricultural produce for winter and accommodation, which meant extra sleeping space for younger siblings in the family home. One of the respondents reported that she had to work as a goose minder at the age of seven. Her parents had seven children and a two-and-a-half hectare farm where they grew rye and potatoes. They worked as servants for richer farmers' and received remuneration in kind. Sometimes they received a basket of pears or plums – the 'Lubka' variety – for their work. One respondent recollects that *there were six of us, and we pounced like hyenas on these plums, and they were gone in a flash. When mother sent us to work as servants, my sister received three metres of rye during summer season, for cattle minding, and I also got three metres of rye. And two metres of potatoes, or a metre, and usually five ridges, a hundred metres long. And we had to dig the crops up* (DX/3). This is how life 'as servants' looked: *In the morning I had to take cows to pasture, and she* [the farmer's wife] *cut a piece of bread and dunked it in milk, like that, and then gave it to me. So I took it and went to work, without breakfast, without anything but this piece of bread soaked in milk. On Saturday evening I went home, where my mother washed me. Sometimes I had so many lice that my hair stood up. The employers found servants repulsive. For instance, my brother was referred to as a farm-hand, and he had to sleep in a horse barn. I remember that at that time I was minding cows, and he came to me, I was near a road with the cows, and he said, 'Danusia, take a look and see if the flies did not pooh on me'. So I told him, 'You are all covered in pooh', because he had slept in the barn, which was full of the flies. There was no other place for servants. I slept according to the same arrangement, usually in the kitchen. When I served at the S.'s, I slept on a bed in the kitchen, but for instance at the K.'s, there was a bench in the kitchen, a bench for sitting, and* [the farmer's wife] *got the bench ready for me, putting some things on it, fur coats, no pillow, then she covered me with something, and that is how I used to sleep. At the L.'s I slept behind a couch. However, I do not remember what she used to put on it. I know that they slept in one bed, and they had two children – who slept in the other bed, and I was sleeping behind the couch* [on the floor] (DX/3).

As a result, the childhood of the oldest generation of women is a period which they recollect as a time with little spare time they could spend on playing. A road and meadows were the only places where children could play. Nature determined the available options. *We had no toys, no one had a toy, we only had some pieces of broken dishes, which we used to take to sandy places to make sandcastles, when I was older, I made ragdolls to play with, we had no dolls from shops, as there was no money for that* (Q/3). *Winters were great, as there were meadows in our village, and when they were soaked with water, we were skating on the ice until the moon rose. After work, when everything was done and it became dark, we used to go to the road, where we were playing hide and seek, or dodgeball, and we had fun. I remember that we were very poor then, but we had fun. People were not as sad as they are nowadays since they have nothing to do. We always had something to do. A big poplar tree was growing near our house, and my brother made a nest for storks on it. The storks were coming and clattering for us, and we were happy because that meant the storks were arriving, everyone was taking their clogs off and ran barefoot, because the storks had arrived, and because it got warm. We were very poor, but we had a lot of fun* (F/3).

1.2. Poverty in childhood in Łódź

Poverty experienced in childhood is also characteristic of the women who grew up in Łódź. Some of the respondents came to Łódź with their families before the WWII, or in one case, a fifteen year old girl came to the city alone to search for work (see Chapter 6, the F. family). These respondents' parents decided to leave the countryside and emigrate to Łódź to search for a better life in the 1920s and early 1930s. They were hoping to improve their difficult material living conditions, to escape poverty and to find work. Łódź was perceived as a city which offered opportunities for work in textile factories and cotton mills. Sometimes the decision to leave the countryside resulted from accidents (for example a fire that destroyed all of a family's property): *My parents had a farm that they had inherited from their parents, they had a house, but they lost everything in a fire. Father put us onto a wagon, as there were many children, and they were all very little, I was also little then, and the youngest sister and our mum were ill, and so we came from the countryside to the city. We lived at my aunt's in her apartment, later we received* [rented] *an apartment, and since then only our family lived there* (O/3). Sometimes family conflicts and misunderstandings accelerated the decision to migrate to Łódź. *Mother-in-law moved into my parents' and my mum could not stand her* – a respondent reports the reasons which contributed to their arrival in Łódź. *Mother-in-law liked alcohol and she used to drink with my father, she also incited him to argue with mum, and finally mum decided to leave him. But since it had put him in a bad light, he left the village, and together with mum and four children, they moved to Łódź* (D/3). After their arrival in Łódź, the living standard was not much better, although the respondents seldom mention the fact that during childhood they had to work in Łódź to earn a living. *When I was at school, I was given cod liver oil because I was badly undernourished. And when I was going to my First Communion, I remember that the neighbours provided the clothes for me, this shows how poor we were* (O/3).

Families that came to Łódź without any financial resources had to stay with their relatives or in rented one-room apartments, which were usually in the attics of small, timber-made tenement houses, in the poorest parts of the city where mostly Jewish population lived. They did not have running water, and the toilet would be an outside privy, for use by all of the residents. The apartments were small, cold, humid and dark, and without sewerage systems. Due to their being part of a very small residential area, they were supplied with basic equipment only. There were cases where not all family members had their own place to sleep. 2–3 persons often had to share one bed. One of the respondents, whose parents were former peasants and decided to move to Łódź with their four children in 1934, remember it in the following way; she was four at the time: *The room had about 15 square metres, there were two beds and a wardrobe, and that was all, the apartment was in the attic, so in summer it was swarming with insects, such as black cockroaches and bedbugs, so our parents moved the beds to the centre to protect us from insect bites. Because there were quite a few children and they were all little. And when winter came, the beds had to be moved again, because the walls were covered with ice and the ice layer was so thick that the beds' sides froze to the wall, and we had to scrape the ice off to move it. So you can imagine how cold that room was.*

Coal was purchased in buckets, per kilogram. When mum bought 5 to10 kilos and brought it home, it was hardly enough to cook a meal. Therefore everything froze, water froze in the apartment and we lived in such conditions until the war, throughout the occupation, and only after the war we moved here, to Ceglana Street, and we still live in this apartment (D/3). *The conditions were very hard as we lived in Bałuty then, there was no electricity and we did homework using an oil lamp* (ZB/3). *We had to carry water from Bałucki Market, there were no water carts, and only in 1946 I had to arrange the connection to warm water and the water supply system myself* (D/3). A permanent fear of eviction accompanied the bad housing conditions: *Mum was saying that she had to pay 40 zloty for that* [rent], *and that was very expensive. We were buying food using coupons or credit transactions, and if our parents managed to earn some funds working as servants, first they had to pay the rent or else they would be evicted by the landlady, and that was it. She* [the landlady] *wouldn't wait. First you had to earn to pay the rent, and only then could the rest be spent on food* (D/3).

After their arrival in Łódź, in most families only the fathers worked and fulfilled the role of chief income earners. Without any vocational qualifications and education, they were only able to find poorly paid work as blue-collar workers in textile factories, or temporary work in the construction sector. *My daddy was an ordinary blue-collar worker, he had no vocational qualifications, he could neither read nor write. Mum was the same. She could neither write nor read* (C/3). The difficult financial status of the respondents' families of origin deteriorated significantly at the time of the economic recession at the end of the 1920s/early 1930s, when their fathers were made redundant. Growing unemployment between 1929 and 1933 was also an effect of the economic crisis[4]. Many factories were liquidated, and many cut down the number of their employees. The fathers who lost their job, lost their regular source of income. They went to work in the morning, and were made redundant in the evening. Seasonal

4 This unemployment was due to significantly reduced production levels and redundancies in the textiles, leather, metallurgical and metal industries; the level of remuneration for employed workers was also reduced. Unfavourable amendments were introduced to the social insurance system, disease benefits were reduced and the duration of payments was shortened. The extent of medical services was also limited (such as the right to obtain medical services by family members of the insured worker), and maternity benefits were reduced too. The situation in the countryside was also difficult. Reduced prices of agricultural products significantly lowered the income available to families there, and the situation of agricultural workers also deteriorated. No work and the low level of income available to the unemployed resulted in difficulties meeting nutritional and housing needs (Landau, Tomaszewski 1981: 220).

work in summer or temporary employment were the only ways to earn money. In the interwar period of 1929–1933, i.e. during the Great Depression, in Łódź the respondents' fathers could only find temporary work in the construction sector, as builders, bricklayers or carpenters, while in the winter season they remained unemployed. *Initially my father worked as a bricklayer, later it was difficult to find work, just like nowadays, so he only did some seasonal work, and at other times he used to go to the so-called 'bigiel'* [a 'big gathering' in Łódź jargon], *there was one in Bałucki Market, where all the unemployed used to come, and an owner would employ them to unload coal, or they were sent to do some work for Jewish entrepreneurs. That is how they used to work* (D/3). Men did temporary work, which provided them with an ad-hoc income. For instance, by helping chopping wood, carrying luggage, making shoes or doors. *My dad only did seasonal work, as he was a woodworker and a carpenter, and mum did not work at all. I remember how we were waiting for Saturday for daddy to come home, so we were waiting outside the gate because daddy was always bringing a large loaf of bread. My daddy was good, he cared and wanted the best for us, he brought us up very well, we were modest, he did not beat us and we were very obedient, but there was no work,* [when he had work] *he used to bring black pudding, the thick type* (O/3). Sometimes their financial status was additionally deteriorated by the fathers' illness. In the winter season, families lived on social benefits – i.e. unemployment insurance – and state benefits, which were available to some.[5] *In winter, when father had no work, the whole family lived on state benefits. After winter, father did some seasonal work again, and in winter, he stayed at home again. We received coupons to get food from a cooperative, so we were never hungry, they gave us coffee and sugar and soap, and soap powder, and when my sister was little, we also received coupons for milk. So we used to go there with a can to bring milk, and get food, including cooked meals, because cooked*

5 This benefit resulted from the law on redundancy insurance of 1924, and was paid by the Unemployment Fund, which was established for this purpose. Pursuant to this law, workers aged over 18 who worked for at least 20 weeks in companies liable for payment of this benefit in the preceding year, were eligible to receive it. This constituted 30% of the remuneration for a single individual and was paid for 13 weeks. The unemployed with families to support received higher benefits, reaching up to 50% of their remuneration in the case of families with seven members. In subsequent years, this law was amended on several occasions, the criteria to grant the benefit was modified, and its amount was systematically reduced. Due to the significant shortage of funding for payment of unemployment benefits, the Supreme Committee for Unemployment was established in 1931 to provide temporary benefits, distribute food, fuel and run cheap canteens for the unemployed, as well as to organise school breakfasts for the children of the unemployed (Hrebenda 1996: 123).

meals were also available. So the state always helped us during these four or five worst months (D/3). However the benefits were only available to the insured. Soup kitchens, or 'cheap canteens' (a term used in reports by the Łódź City Board), which distributed free soup, were commonly available to the unemployed. They were funded under the city budget and operated in all city districts. However, there were separate facilities for blue-collar workers and white-collar workers (Warzywoda-Kruszyńska 1999).

1.2.1. Working mothers. Caring for younger siblings

Assuming chores and co-responsibility for caring for younger siblings at a young age is a characteristic experience of the oldest respondents who spent their childhood in Łódź. *I was looking after children all day long* (W/3) is how one of the respondents concluded the description of her childhood. The eldest sister was responsible for caring for her siblings when her father was unemployed and her mother, who had to look for work and assumed responsibility for maintaining the family, was away from home. *Laundry, housework, seasonal work in the countryside, inhumanely exploited home-based work, and selling agricultural products represent only a few of the women's chores* (Jażdżyńska 1958: 25). In 1935, Anna Minkowska reported the living conditions of the unemployed in the period of the most severely reduced employment (end of 1930/beginning of 1931), and this is how she wrote about the woman's role in poor families: *Women borrow money to buy goods on credit in stores. Although the average value of her (the woman's) income is lower than the income of the head of the family, the burden and care of the family maintenance primarily fell on the woman – wife and mother. She demonstrates an amazing energy and inventiveness in finding sources of income: laundry, cleaning, sewing, small-scale street trading, gardening, etc. She is trying to secure the family budget doing all kinds of temporary work (not many women have regular work at factories or other enterprises). And when she is no longer able to find these classic sources of a woman's temporary income, it is she who is mostly responsible for accomplishing the hard task of obtaining assistance in the form of support and gifts from family, loans from friends, support from the social security services, Kropla Mleka*[6] *from Charity Associations, and she neither gives up nor laments. She assumes the duties of the family breadwinner with dignity and understanding, and combines them with upkeep of the family, which is a tough task in such conditions. Woman – wife, woman – mother is the family member who sustains the full impact of the failure of unemployment and its consequences* (Minkowska 1996: 106). The author's

6 Kropla Mleka (A Drop of Milk) – a charity organisation that cared for the nutrition of infants.

observations are confirmed in the reports of our respondents: *In the hard times, mummy left five of us at home to search for work again. She either went to do the laundry or went cleaning for Jewish families, and came back home in the evening, and we were simply waiting for food. That was such a hard life, unfortunately. That is how life used to be before the war. When mum cooked a meal once a day, she gave us a lot to eat, to make sure that we had enough. So when she went to the 'bigiel' in the morning, she could earn some money by doing laundry or cleaning for a Jewish family, and she came back in the evening, and the Jewish woman knew that my mother had small children so she gave her more food. And if she did not know, she paid money, and then we got fed the following day. That was our life. We were poor, poor, very poor* (D/3).

1.3. World War II and the Nazi-German occupation

The outbreak of World War II was of formative significance to the women of the oldest generation. The Occupation significantly impacted their biographies and significantly determined attitudes they adopted in their mature life. This generation of women was growing older *at an accelerated rate,* assuming the role of the person responsible for providing for the mother and younger siblings, particularly when the father was deported to Germany. The outbreak of the war interrupted their education, *I was in my fourth year at school when the war started and I could not continue education* (I/3). Only few women completed elementary school before the outbreak of the war. Most of them started school in the years just before the outbreak, and in September 1939, they were the first year pupils of elementary school. In the initial months of the war, the Łódź Occupation Authorities decided to close Polish schools, and only in 1943, three vocational schools, which were to prepare Polish youth for work, were organised. Girls were mainly trained to meet the needs of the German clothing and textile industry. The training was limited to teaching them specific job-oriented activities, which would be useful for work in Germany or in German enterprises in Łódź. Some of the respondents attended elementary schools for children aged 9 to 14, where they studied for three days, then had to work for three days (Bojanowski 1992: 129–141).

The women remember the Occupation as a time of fear, hunger, displacement, deportation to work in Germany, and hard work. *Those were very sad years, I would not like to live through them again, and although I was a little child then, I remember that we were living under constant fear as you never knew whether they would come to make us homeless or not. Sometimes the Gestapo were raiding homes all night long. We had everything packed, in case of displacement* (Q/3). The Occupation was a time when they experienced food shortages, and sometimes hunger. As early as in the initial months of the war, Łódź ran out of almost all basic food products. The Occupation Authorities introduced food rationing, and in May 1941, a coupon-based scheme which covered almost all food products. The quantity of the allocated food decreased systematically and was insufficient to meet peoples' needs. The options for complementing small food rations with food purchased on the free market were also limited, due to high prices in particular. In such circumstances, obtaining extra food products was only possible as a result of mutual help and direct purchases made in the countryside. The shortage of basic food products was experienced throughout the Occupation (Bojanowski 1992: 165–176). Potatoes, bread and soup made of turnips were often the only available food. Children who lived in the countryside were in a little bit better situation. In most cases, remuneration for work for German farmers was 'paid' in the form of food. *When* [mum] *worked for that farmer, he gave her milk, cream, bread and butter. That specific German farmer always helped* (E/3). Families also found other ways to complement food rations: *Bread was often rationed* (at home), *you needed coupons to get it, and there were many children in our family, parents had a hand mill hidden under a straw layer and they also had some grain, so mum baked bread from the grain, it was coarse and dark* (Q/3).

1.3.1. Displacement and forced labour in Germany

In accordance with the occupying forces' policy of colonisation and displacement, families that lived in the countryside were displaced from their farms and deported to work in Germany, with Germans settling in the acquired farms. *The war came, and they displaced us, there was no farming activity during the German Occupation as they took our land from us* (I/3). *Large farm owners were forced to leave their farms and were moved to Germany to work there. Almost everyone was gone, and Germans settled here* (Q/3). Initially only men were deported for forced labour, i.e. the fathers and brothers of the respondents, who were teenagers at the time. Over 30,000 people were deported from Łódź to the Reich for forced labour in May and June 1940. *Father was deported to Germany, and mother had to work at the German farmer's on her own, to provide for all of us* (E/3), one of the respondents reports. *In 1942, during the Occupation, father was deported to Germany to work, in May, and after his deportation, my mum gave birth to the third child in October, and she had to work until father's return* (W/3), the other respondent reports. The following cases also happened: *Father and mother were deported to Germany, and I had no life, nothing, we had to eat dry bread* (N/3). Germans only occupied land owned by wealthier Polish farmers. *Not everyone was displaced, we had a little less land, so they decided to leave us, as they also needed people to do the work* (Q/3). The group of employees recruited by Germans also included children: *I was thirteen years old* – one of the respondents reports – *when I had to work as a servant to Germans. I worked on a farm since 1940 until 1945, I was a child minder, they had three children, I also had to graze cows, do housework, and work in the field. I had to do everything there* (I/3). Another respondent adds: *I was minding cows of German farmers to earn some money* (Q/3).

The youngest children who were deported to Germany for forced labour were 14 years old. Our respondents were also involved in 'the Labour': *I was 15 years old when they deported me to Germany*, one declared. Another respondent presents more details: *Many of us were taken then, they deported us, moved us to a bath, males and females were in the same room to have a bath, and we were embarrassed as we were still children. And then a German hit us with a rubber baton, and we had swollen bruises. And I was deported to Germany. I stayed at a farmer's in Mecklenburg. The food was very good, but the work was never-ending. I had to wake up in the morning at one to milk cows, 15 cows, so my hands were in so much pain that it kept me awake at night, after milking the cows – breakfast, washing up* [the dishes], *I had to clean the stove, and go to work in the field. The work in winter was also hard, I had to distribute manure in the field* (B/3). Another respondent reports: *In 1941, in June, I was sent to Germany, I had just turned 15, and they needed young people so they kept me. I was serving at a farmer's in Germany, I was even sent to very good people, an elderly couple. They did not have their own children, their only son was in the army. So I worked at their farm. I stayed there until 1945 and returned (to Poland) in February 1945, and started work right away, in March* (ZB/3). The respondents that managed to avoid compulsory deportation to work in Germany were able to do so thanks to the assistance of relatives, friends and even Germans who had lived in Poland before the war, and who issued statements to confirm that the respondents had been employed.

Displacement from apartments was also an experience shared by those who lived in Łódź during the Occupation. During the process of establishing the Jewish Ghetto, residents of the territory assigned to the Jewish population were made to leave their apartments. *Just after Christmas, they told us to move out immediately, and that was when the Germans established the ghetto, the ghetto was there all the time, in the Bałuty district, and we had to look for another apartment ourselves* (ZB/3).

1.3.2. Working in German factories. Taking responsibility for the mother and younger siblings

Just after the war began, the number of Łódź textile factories was significantly reduced, and so was the number of employees, too. Large-scale unemployment began. Confiscated machinery and most of the textile resources were moved to Germany. Clothes-making factories, which mainly manufactured uniforms and clothes for the needs of the army, replaced the liquidated textile mills. The Germans founded Labour Offices, which registered the people who were able to work, and determined the place of their employment. They also organised deportations of Poles to Germany. In 1942, they experienced shortages in the labour force for the first time, and applied the obligation of forced labour to people aged over 14, in that year in Łódź. This obligation was also applied to women who had small children. The respondents' mothers had to go to work. When their mothers were working, they had to do the housework and care for their younger siblings. *My childhood was very sad as I had to look after children all day long, mummy was at work all day long. She left home when it was dark, and came back when it was dark, so I had this feeling that she was away all day long. And I stayed with the children, with the help of an aunt or grandma, as they popped round to see how I was doing, but it was still my responsibility. In 1943 I was 13, 14 years old, and that was my duty, well, my obligation to look after the children and cook something, obviously something with milk for the smallest ones. And I was always saying that quite often I grabbed a bucket with garbage, when mum was back home, and went out to dispose it, to empty the bucket, and that was when I could do all the running. I even grabbed our caretaker's shovel to shovel snow off in the street, I was so happy being outside in the fresh air. And I know that once, when I got back home, mummy said to me: O my God, your cheeks are so red, what did you do, who was nasty to you, and my face was so purple because of the happiness that I could be outside for such a long time* (W/3).

The forced labour was only for those who were able to work and were over 14, however school children aged between 10 and 11 were also forced to work in German clothing factories. The share of working children aged under 14 in the total number of those employed at different plants ranged from 5% to 12% of the total labour force. They worked for the same number of hours, also did night shifts, and in many cases had to do the same jobs as the adults (Bojanowski 1992: 262–270). Reports by our respondents indicate that some of them were sent to work in German clothing factories: *In 1942, the Germans took me to a school, I was a pupil at the German school for 6 weeks, they were probably preparing me for deportation, but later I fell ill with scarlet fever and stayed in a hospital in Julianów, and never went back to this school, and after I left the hospital*

I was taken to a factory and I worked in this factory's spinning mill until the liberation (D/3). *I started to work when I was 11 years old, at Wulle's factory, because mummy was ill, daddy was serving in the army, so was my brother, my younger sister stayed at home at the time, so I had to maintain the family almost all by myself, I was working for 12 hours, from 6 am to 6 pm, but my salary was good under the German occupation. You had to use coupons for everything, but I could afford to buy the coupons, smoked sausage, frankfurters, and mortadella were the only available cold meats, but I always bought them, and we had them, as I worked for many hours and earned a lot* (O/3).

2. Youth

2.1. Starting work in a factory – a new biographical experience

The end of the war marked another phase in the lives of the oldest respondents, i.e. the phase of hard, multi-year work, and in many cases, overall responsibility for the family that was imposed on the teenage respondents, when their parents – the mothers in particular – were unable to work due to their poor health, or had died. *In 1952, my father was ill for three weeks and then died. Mum stayed with us, I was 17, and my brother 14. Mummy did not work anywhere as she was scared of factories, she only did some seasonal work in summer, we had a cow and that was how we lived, with my mother* (H/3).

After the war, forced labourers, including our respondents, came back home. They usually returned at a time just after Poland's territory had been consequently occupied by the Red Army. *When the Russians came in January 1945, we gathered together with several Poles who were still there, it was in the morning, and we agreed to go back, everyone to their home town. The return took a very long time, two weeks in my case. We got lost as we went the wrong way, and even the men didn't know the right direction either, and a battlefront was still there. It took me about two weeks to reach my place in Łódź* (ZB/3). Opportunities to learn became available, however the women did not continue their education and went to work instead. *After I returned from Germany, I had to search for work, I am not even sure whether I completed Year 7 when I started to search for work. If my family had been normal, i.e. if I had not had to work, I would have gone to school, but in our family we had to earn to survive as our family was big. Dad was unable to earn enough, and each one of us had to go and earn our living ourselves, well, maybe I could study in an evening school, but since I gave up, I lost my ambition and did not think of school, I was only thinking of work, I did not think what I should do later, you do not think about such things when you are young. Only work, work, work, and if you had work, your life was good, so people did not think of school, only work mattered. No one wanted to employ me since only over 18-year-olds were allowed to work, and I had to work so I lied that I was two years older and started work in a sewing room* (O/3). *I was 15 or 16 years old, I cannot remember, anyway, I was not old enough and they did not want to employ me, however my father worked there and issued his consent that I should help him there a little* (E/3). This economic obligation destroyed the educational aspirations of those who wanted to do jobs other than a factory worker's: *I had the intention to learn, I was dreaming of becoming a nurse, but life forced me to work. I had to go to work, my mum was very ill after the war, daddy came back from those trenches* [forced labour], *and the elder siblings, we had to go to work, we had to help our father to maintain the family. If you were older, you started work and you worked, and later you didn't feel like* [going to school], *when I turned 20, I got married and my life changed, and I no longer felt like going to school* (D/3).

For girls from the countryside, the decision to move to Łódź was an event that significantly influenced their future lives. *I could not count on anyone's help, I knew that I had to work, I had no other option, it was pointless to think of further education. Everyone left* [the countryside] *as soon as they were old enough to search for work, those who were already in the city helped others to join them* (Q/3). Some respondents stayed with their relatives: *I came to Łódź in 1949. First to my aunt's. She was a clothes maker so I was helping her a little to get food, and later I went to work* (I/3), while others' destinations were unplanned: *I left for Legnica to learn in a vocational school. I insisted, I knew that there was no future for me there* [in the countryside], *I had to acquire some skills, simply to be able to work. After the graduation, there was a job allocation process, and together with a friend we chose Łódź, later we regretted that decision, but we chose Łódź and we stayed in Łódź* (Q/3).

After the end of the WWII, 70% of Łódź's industrial capacity was available again, and production was launched under two- and three-shift systems. In 1948, industry regained its full pre-war production capacity (Marczyńska-Witczak 1996). Thus, the respondents commenced employment as teenage girls and continued until retirement. *I started working in a spinning mill when I was 17, and stayed there for 34 years* (D/3). *I came back* [from Germany] *in February, and already in March I started work, I was working and learning a little as I did not have any skills, but I acquired them there and continued working in the spinning mill, I worked for 27 years as an overlock operator* (ZB/3). Their employment in a factory was a turning point in the lives of many of the respondents, a critical point that in their opinion marked a significant improvement of their financial status: *Life was not luxurious, quite often I cooked potatoes for our meals, and everyone got a piece of sausage on Sunday. We did not have much, but at least we did not go to bed feeling hungry, and that was most important* (F/3). *Some days were better, others were harder, but we were never hungry again* (C/3). *I was a young lass, we had our own 'young people's conveyor belt', I produced a lot, received bonuses, awards, my earnings at the spinning mill were very good, I did well. I was happy with my job, I liked it very much, modest life, but I had enough money, and I even sent things to my mum, sometimes I would buy oranges to send them to my mum* (Q/3).

Most of the respondents spent their whole working life in one company. *I was always working in the spinning mill, under a three-shift system, in one company from the beginning to the end, for 35 years* (B/3). They worked for 35 years on average. Several respondents worked for over forty years, and one even completed 50 years of service. They worked under two- or three-shift systems. *We worked for two shifts in the spinning mill, from 5 am to 1 pm. Then from 2 pm, or 1.30 pm until 9.30 pm, and later I worked at a university, and somehow I completed my 50 years of service in total, and I also had some occasional work, and I was doing my best and I coped somehow* (ZB/3). *For me there was only work and work, from work and to work* – the same respondent sums up her life (ZB/3).

3. Adulthood

3.1. Getting married

After several years of work, at the end of the 1940s/early 1950s, the respondents began getting married. None of them were teenage wives, being at least twenty when they started their families. In accordance with the standard that was binding at the time, their partners were older than the respondents and belonged to the same social class. They had completed elementary school at most, and were blue-collar workers in the same textile factories, working as carpenters, bricklayers, drivers or electricians. Young people usually met at work, during various events organised by the management or youth organisations for the employees. They married after a brief 'dating' period, which usually lasted several months. The calling-up of men for military service accelerated the matrimonial decision. *I got married in 1951. My husband did military service, as this took place during his military service. There was nothing rushing him, however he was afraid that I would not wait for him. That is why our wedding was a helter skelter event* (W/3). *Husband joined the army in 1948, we did not have children, he came back from the army in 1950, and then it started, I had four children* (ZB/3).

Just after the wedding my husband joined the army, he served for three years. When I got married I didn't have any children, then my husband came back, there was one son, then the other, I stopped working for 8 years to raise our children (O/3). Marriage for women of this generation lasted 32 years on average. There was no engagement party prior to the wedding as their parents lived far away, there was no money, and maybe there was no such custom in the countryside. None of the respondents recalls such a celebration or receiving a ring from their fiancés. They also do not mention a situation where the fiancé would ask the parents for permission to marry their daughter. It seems that in the study group, marriage was treated as the young couple's business, while their parents, if possible, assisted to organise the wedding. If the ceremony was held in the countryside, it was likely that the parent's involvement was greater: *Family helped to organise our wedding in the countryside, I bought my wedding outfit with my own money* (Q/3). Wedding receptions were very modest and were held at home. *My wedding was a very modest event, maybe with 10 guests* (L/3). When today's grandmothers were getting married, the law required that prior to a church wedding, the couple had to be married in a Registry Office. Some respondents decided to have only the civil law ceremony, which was a violation of the general standard that required couples to be married in church, in accordance with the catholic religion. *We could not afford to buy outfits for this* [church] *wedding, so we had the civil law wedding, and only when Mirusia was going to the First Communion, we wanted to change this because the child was always asking questions, why mummy did not have a church wedding photo, so we got married, in December at Christmas, such a quiet and modest wedding, and Mirusia's Communion was in May* (W/3).

At the beginning of their married lives, the respondents had low economic capital, which was not significantly expanded through presents from family and guests. *We received some wedding presents, and we had to earn* [for] *ourselves to buy the rest* (Q/3). *My husband and I had to earn everything* (B/3). *We were doing our best, starting from a fork, a plate, and a bed* (T/3).

Parents gave me what they could, a spoon, a bowl, and something to sleep on, later on, my husband and I changed everything in this apartment (C/3).

In their adulthood, matrimonial relations became the key determinant of their further lives, as well as critical points in the biographies of their children. The quality of their marriage was inter-related with the families' living standard and style, which also determined the cultural, economic and social capital they passed to their children. The key demarcation line was whether the man they chose for a husband was, or would become, a heavy drinker or alcoholic. This fact was significant to organisation of the family life (child raising, reconciling professional and family duties, relations with grandchildren), as well as the living situation of these women in their elderly years. The following types of matrimonial relations, which further impacted the course of the respondents' lives, can be identified in the study group:

1. Partner relations – both partners work outside, share household duties, and take care of the children,
2. Traditional relations – the husband works; the wife takes care of household and children when they are young,
3. Relations without trust – the husband works but spends all the money on alcohol, the wife works in a factory and does extra work to meet the household and children's needs.

The first two types of matrimonial relations provided living stability at a modest level, while the third involved a permanent fight by the women to survive.

In all these cases, it was incidental events that constituted the circumstances leading to poverty. Sometimes an event was of such traumatic significance that it set the family, who used to cope well in the past, on a trajectory of poverty.

3.2. Reconciling work with maternity and child care

3.2.1. Marriages founded on partner relations

It was common for couples to have children born after their parents married, which was in accordance with social norms. This represents a key characteristic of this generation. The respondents were all workers, so reconciling work with childcare was of the utmost importance. At the time the respondents had their own children, maternity leave lasted 8–12 weeks, and there was no specific childcare leave. In the marriages founded on partnership relations, both parents, who usually just 'passed each other' at home, shared childcare duties. This was possible for workers employed in shifts.. *My husband was working one shift, and I did the other, and that is how we raised our children, I enrolled the son to nursery, and then to kindergarten* (B/3).

My husband and I did shift work, he worked three shifts and so did I. I was very lucky, he was a good man, he did laundry and even cooked lunches when I was at work, I was starting work in the morning, and he worked night and afternoon shifts, so I had lunch ready, even when he was on a disability leave, he cooked lunches and I had everything, I almost had nothing to do (N/3). *I could not complain, my husband cooked lunches, cleaned the house, did laundry and ironing, fed the children, we did our best to make sure that someone always stayed with the children, collected them from kindergarten and addressed their learning needs* (T/3). In the marriages founded on partner relations things were done in accordance with need, not gender.

3.2.2. Traditional marriages

The division of roles in traditional marriages was clearly defined. The working husband maintained the family financially, while his wife took care of the houshold and children. Women from families in which the family's financial situation was relatively good decided to suspend their professional careers after giving birth to their children. Money was sufficient to meet the family's needs as the father's earnings were sufficient, and in addition to his regular salary he also brought in money with extra work, so-called odd jobs. The lack of relatives who could help with childcare supported the couple's decision to have the mother stay at home with the children. *When I had the second child in 1959, my husband and I had almost no one left, grandma died, parents did not live in Łódź, husband worked as a painter and I stayed at home after I had given birth to the other child. I did not work for 9 years* (W/3).

My husband could not live without work, another respondent reports. *He was working day and night. Quite often, just before 4 am, five minutes to four he used to lay down on the carpet, stretch his arms, stretch all his body, then get up and go to work.* Her daughter adds: *Dad came back for lunch, and after lunch he went back to work, as he did some extra work apart from his regular employment. He was either building houses, installing windows or floors* (F/1). The traditional division of roles in the family was not permanent. Once the children reached kindergarten age, respondents went back to work, but not to the factory. Instead, they worked as cleaners, kitchen assistants, janitors and caretakers, thus they chose such jobs that did not require working in shift.

3.2.3. Lack of trust in marital relations – alcoholism in the family of procreation

The respondents in this study, from the 'grandmother' generation, did not provide detailed accounts of facts and the emotions they experienced when they had to share their lives with men who were notorious drinkers.

However, more detail is reported by their daughters. The oldest women that shared their lives with alcoholics or heavy drinkers usually said that they could not rely on their husbands, and that they had to get extra work to maintain the children, that they had to ask other people for help and that they were short of money. They never mentioned violence, police interventions, neglected children. However, they often mention their neurosis, hyperactivity, lack of confidence, and apathy. When the husband was drinking, the wife could not rely on him and had to arrange childcare, so that she could get extra work to compensate the lacking husband's income. In those circumstances the inter-generational assistance of women, which was described by Daniel Bertaux (1995), and Elżbieta Tarkowska in the context of the post-state agricultural enterprise [PGR] communities in Poland, became invaluable. This is how one of the respondents describes her mother-in-law's help looking after her children: *I was raising four children, and my husband loved drinking, had a hard life. But my mother-in-law was so good that she took one child to live with her, although her living standard also was not high, but she took him and cared for him until he reached almost school-age. Then I had the second child, and she also raised it as I had to work all the time, and then I was free and I could go to work and come back from work, and when I could I would care for the children, and my mother-in-law helped me. When I had the fourth son, she came to us every day at 6 am, I would go to work, and she stayed with the children* (ZB/3). When there were no relatives to look after the children, the respondents looked for help from their neighbours, friends, senior women who looked after babies, and then fellow kindergarten parents and pupils. They did so under the promise of mutual assistance or for a small fee, when the mother was working in a factory, or did some extra work in exchange. *I could no longer rely on my husband, so I had that lady who collected children from kindergarten and fed them when I was at work, I prepared everything myself* (Q/3).

3.3. Financial conditions of the family of procreation

The financial conditions of the women who lived in 'normal' marriages became stable at a level free of financial risk. After several years of intensive work, they managed to reach a level of income that provided them with *relative financial stability,* that is, a level sufficient to meet their ongoing daily needs. Families without alcoholic members did not suffer from major financial crises. The women recall that it was in the late 1960s that for the first time, they were able to spend holidays away from home, buy new household equipment, new furniture and renovate their apartments. *When the summer holidays started, and when the children were young, we used to go to Mazury* [Lake District], *or to the seaside* (D/3). They had to make additional effort to raise the income to meet major needs, pay for summer holidays, purchase more valuable assets, and pay for children's education. Then they took extra jobs, took loans or bought things in instalments. *If we had to buy something more expensive, we used to incur loans, if we were going on holidays, we had to incur loans to spend those two weeks with the children. When, for instance, I was sending my son to a technical secondary school, I had to sell some gold jewellery to get him a uniform to ensure that when he went to school he looked decent, in the past schoolchildren had to wear uniforms, every schoolchild had one. And if you could not afford it, you had to incur a loan, not to be afraid of people, as we used to say* (D/3). *When you wanted to buy something, for your apartment, your stomach had to wait. If we wanted to buy something for us, for the children, or something for the apartment, it was obvious that we had to buy everything in instalments* (E/3).

Families with alcoholics had no financial stability, as a chronic lack of money was a result of alcoholism. Accepting gifts and incurring debts was a way of obtaining the necessary goods and money to complement the funds earned through regular employment. Palska (1999, 2000) observed that borrowing happens only in the face of actual necessity, and is used to meet elementary needs. It generates a permanent feeling of threat, a fear that the family will be unable to repay the loan, and a fear that they will become insolvent. It carries unpleasant psychological consequences, and creates the worrying circumstance of *living in debt* – the need to incur new liabilities to repay the previous ones. When the respondents' families ran out of money, those married to alcoholics had to try to get a loan or a gift: One daughter reports: *My mum could never rely on father to bring money home. When she had no money, she used to get money or food from her sister, or she always had to borrow from someone, mum had a very wealthy sister, so we quite often went to see her, and she gave mum, not lent, she gave food and money, and if she did not, mum always borrowed from someone* (Z/1). Employers, who at that time had a statutory duty to render quasi-financial/banking services to employees, were also a significant support. It was the only available form of borrowing money to some women: *I was incurring small payday loans from each employer, I did not manage to repay one before already incurring another, and as it happened, everyone was understanding* (ZB/3).

However the key method of obtaining money was the respondents' extra jobs: *I managed somehow, I used to work in a sewing room, and I additionally worked at another place, it's really no shame, but someone always guaranteed for me. I used to clean wealthier people's apartments. I had to submit a short CV. I normally would go there after work at the sewing room or in the morning, for an hour or two, I did shopping, I had to vacuum clean the apartment, clean it, sometimes I cooked lunch, it was not hard work for me, I worked there for two years and that is how I made ends meet* (ZB/3). The same respondent also worked as a kitchen assistant during wedding receptions. Sometimes extra job was available from their regular employer: *When I worked at the school and did not earn enough money for my full-time work, I additionally accepted a part-time job to clean classrooms, and in that way I earned extra money, I did the same when I worked at kindergarten, full-time job started at 7 am and finished at 3 pm, and additionally I was a night caretaker of the kindergarten to earn extra money* (O/3). She also worked during holidays, which allowed her to ensure holidays away from the city for her children: *I knew a farmer in the countryside, I worked there a lot, helped when they had to work in the field, and I stayed with the children, she had three children, and I did the cooking, cleaning, and she could work in the field with peace of mind* (O/3). The women who stopped working to raise small children, who had alcohol addicted husbands that did not fulfil the duty of breadwinner, had to go back to work earlier: *I had to go to work when my sons were no longer babies, and I started working at a kindergarten as a kitchen assistant, because I was awfully nervous and did not want to work again as a machine operator, I wanted to work one shift only, and somewhere closer as I already lived here. I worked at a kindergarten, and the work there was hard, but I worked because I had two sons and my husband left us. I was very happy with that, because my husband was a terrible man, an alcoholic!* (O/3)

3.4. Events that damage stability – illness and husband's death

The illnesses and deaths of the respondents' husbands were important biographical events in the study families. Their problem weakened fragile financial stability, and death significantly reduced the family's income. A daughter of one of the respondents reports: *We always had money as my parents were saving, they were the first to buy a television set of all the neighbours, they bought a plot of land to build a house, but father's disease made them change all the plans, and the plot had to be sold. Father had been working until he became ill, once the illness started, mum had to maintain him* (R/3). Unexpected and costly illness often came at times when the children were getting married. Both types of expenses affected the family resources. *A lot of money was spent on therapy, then we had to save a little as we had to organise the children's weddings* (F/3).

Another respondent reports that her husband's illness and death were the events that marked the point at which their lives became more difficult: *My husband was, somehow I did not realise that he was in such a bad condition, that someone in our family was ill, or that something else hap-*

pened. I had to rush to work in the morning, then I was back, did the shopping, cooked lunch, then off to bed, children to school, we were happy, our life was very good. My husband had a stroke, initially he had a heart attack, developed diabetes, and then just within two years he had the stroke, and that was the end. If he had been alive, our life would have been different. There were two of us, my husband always was at home, he was always helping, life used to be easier than it is now (ZG/3).

The death of a grown-up child was a traumatic experience which influenced the respondents' lives further:

We had such a tragedy in our family, the eldest son died suddenly at home. It was Sunday, we were sitting at the table, and all of a sudden he fell off the couch onto the floor. We called an ambulance, the doctor established that he had had a severe stroke, they took him to a hospital, and he never regained consciousness. That was a dreadful experience for me as he was my first son, the eldest, that was a dreadful experience for me and that was the moment I gave up work as it affected my mental condition badly, his funeral was on Christmas Eve in 1992, that was when my son was buried, and I stopped working (ZB/3).

4. Old age

All of the respondents from the 'grandmother' generation have received old-age or disability pensions since the 1990s. Transformations on the labour market (from the employee market to the employer market), resulting from the system transformation of Poland in 1989, did not directly affect them. However, they did tremendously influence their lives through the fact that their children and grandchildren lost their jobs and their means of living. This is why their divorced daughters, grandchildren and sons moved back into their parents' apartments and began to co-maintain the household. Even when the children lived separately, the 'grandmothers' supported them financially as they were the only family members that had regular income.

4.1. Living on an old age pension in an extended family

Living on a disability pension or retirement pension as a strategy for coping with poverty is characteristic of life in the countryside, and has previously been looked at in the literature (Tarkowska 2000; Laskowska-Otwinowska 1998; Zabłocki 1999; Korzeniewska 2002). *Providing systematic and regular financial assistance to grown-up children creates a characteristic economic relationship of inter-generational dependence, however it also prevents the spread of poverty* (Korzeniewska 2002: 153). In the countryside, the supporting family members usually lived in a separate household. In Łódź, the pensions of the oldest generation of women were an important source of income in the shared households, and sometimes represented the only regular income in the shared family budget. Aggregating all income in the shared family household was the key strategy for coping with poverty. If the shared income was composed of a pension, at least one salary (provided by a son-in-law) and social assistance benefits or child support benefits, the family managed to meet their on going needs. They maintained the family jointly. As one of the women said: *Together we have enough to live on and to pay for these formalities* (fees and charges), *and we are currently coping somehow, living from one payment day to another, we live from the tenth to the tenth* (Z/3). Though income was sufficient to meet ongoing needs, they needed to manage their spending in a sound and economical way. They were unable to save any money, but at the same time they did not have to borrow from others. Some respondents spent all their pensions on maintaining their unemployed, divorced and seriously ill daughters, grandchildren, grown-up single sons, who were unable to get work due to poor health or alcoholism. *I helped my son to raise his children, I also help him now as he is unemployed, I give him what I can. I cannot give him much since I will not have enough money to live on. I never ask people for money, I have to live using the money I have. My pension is 540 zloty. When I help the children, I need to be very economical to last until the next pension payment day, without incurring any loans. I am 68 years old and my life was hard, because I had to work, then raise children, and then my husband died in 1980, and now my life is coming to the end, my age is coming to the end and everything is coming to the end, and that's it* (D/3). *My son is unemployed and I had to pay all the bills, I cannot imagine what would happen if I did not provide him with things, if I did not help. I do not have too much however I share everything with him* (O/3).

My son is currently unemployed and receives social assistance benefit, he is not eligible to receive unemployment benefit as he had not worked for 6 months before registration [at the Employment Office], *he used to work but now there is no work for him, he has been unemployed for several years and stays at home. He has received social assistance benefit for two years now* (ZB/3). *She* [daughter] *is very ill, and does not live with her husband, who left her, and we struggle with the children. She stays at my place all the time, as in her flat there is no electricity, no toilet, and no gas. She had coal but somebody stole it, so she keeps coming to my flat, we cook lunches, and she only goes back to her apartment to sleep, she stays at my place almost all the time, when she gets the family benefit she brings it to me, or when I get my pension, then we go shopping. The son-in-law does not even come to see the children, he is with another woman, and the children do not want to know him, and he does not come to see them so I am with her all the time* (C/3). They were unable to save any funds. *We were able to save in the past, but now it is very difficult. I cannot save a penny, it would be possible if it was only me, and I have to spend money all the time. Sometimes I borrow a little money, then I have to repay it, and then I borrow again as I cannot make ends meet. I need a lot of money to buy medication for my daughter* (C/3).

There was not enough money to buy food: *Sometimes there are better days, sometime worse, quite often the situation is very bad when we have fifteen hundred zloty to maintain 7 people, then you cannot do much and life is so hard then. Sometimes you do not even get a piece* [of meat] *because we cannot afford to buy it as you need a kilo of meat if everyone is going to get a piece. There are days when it is very hard and we cannot even afford to buy bread, well, our life is very hard as there are so many of us, and I have to pay the rent, well I have to pay for everything. And my daughter falls behind with her rent, and she was not paying electricity bills in that previous apartment for 2 or 3 years, so the accrued interest reached two or three thousand. The son-in-law did not give her any money and she could not pay the bills so she was evicted. There is no electricity. She did not pay the electricity bills so the company disconnected the electricity in this apartment too* (C/3).

Another respondent reported that: *Sometimes we are having dry bread, and sometimes I dunk the dry bread in water and then sprinkle it with sugar. If you become hungry, you have lunch at midday, and dinner at 7 pm, and I have nothing to eat in the morning, I only have a coffee and do not have anything to eat until twelve. I am always having coffee and do not have anything to eat, but sometimes I buy half of a pound cake to have with my coffee* (N/3).

4.2. Grandmothers as foster families

The idea of foster families was established to provide 'family' care (instead of care in an orphanage) for children whose biological parents had lost their parental rights. Parents lose these rights if they neglect their duties, which often results from alcoholism or, in rarer cases, mental illness.

One of the respondents described in detail how she became a foster family, after her daughter's husband went to work abroad and the daughter started drinking heavily: *Her husband was good, he completed a secondary technical school and became a cook, he was earning, but he wanted to go to Russia as Poles could go to work there, so he left. When he was gone, she stayed with their child and she was also pregnant with another. As soon as she felt that there was no control, as her husband was not there, she started drinking, and she had companions. When she gave birth, her other child was one year old and it kept being ill all the time, and had to stay in hospital about 15 times. I have all the documentation. I took the child away from her as I was very sorry for him. I took him to my home to raise him. Now the child is 16 years old. In 1983, I applied to the court as I did not get any money for the child. Somebody instructed me to go to a* [welfare] *office, so I went there. I received some child support from the office, but the amount was very small, and it was very hard for me... I met a probation officer, a lady, and she told me that I had to apply to the court to become foster family. She said that I would get money for the child. So I had to apply* (...) *and became his foster family and have been raising him since then* (ZB/3).

Persons fulfilling the role of foster parents receive a specific amount to maintain the child, pursuant to a court order, and this has enabled grandmothers to meet their grandchildren's basic needs. In the study group of fifteen women of the 'grandmothers' generation, four took the status of foster family. Three of these had alcoholic husbands, and their children also abuse alcohol and neglect their own offspring.

4.3. Health problems – lack of money for medical care

Everything would be fine, if we were only healthy. When I was young, I was healthy, and the senior age is the worst as I am ill and cannot earn extra money, and the pension is so small (O/3). Elderly women had different problems with their health, which kept worsening. *I was hardly ever ill, but now I am no longer healthy,* [before] *maybe I had a sick leave once every 2 or 3 years; I was never off sick when I used to work at the university, now I have problems with the liver, the kidneys and with the spine* (...) *but I am taking pills, and I am doing everything I can to feel better. When I was 55 or 56 years old I was healthy, and now I am 71* (ZB/3).

Many years of hard work in a factory as a machine operator induced serious somatic disorders in most of the women interviewed in this study, including backache and cardiac disorders. *I've already stayed at Barlicki hospital 16 times due to cardiac problems* (B/3). *I have been taking medication for my heart for many years as I suffer from hypoxia and circulatory disorders* (W/3). Many of these health problems are rooted in neuroses and depression, resulting from negative emotional experiences. These included financial problems, the related lack of confidence and stability, and silent suffering with the husbands' alcoholism.

The problems of their grown-up children were the most painful emotional experiences such as failed relationships and family lives, as well as unemployment and alcohol abuse. It was hard for these women to deal with the fact that their grandchildren suffered from unsatisfied needs. One of the respondents experienced severe depression, and required permanent psychiatric treatment: *These sad events led to the situation that since March 2 years ago, I have had to be under the regular care of a psychiatrist at a psychiatric clinic* (W/3). These elderly women saved money by not buying the medicine they needed. Thought they are ill themselves, they have to give up buying medicine. *I do not have enough to buy food and medicine*, one respondent notes. *I received a prescription for a medicine to treat my osteoporosis, and the cost was ninety zloty per prescription. So I did not buy it at all as I could not afford it* (I/3). However they always bought drugs for their grown-up children when they became ill, as the lack could put their life at risk.

4.4. Summing up one's life – subjective assessment of one's life in the past and at present

The elderly women interviewed in this study were very critical of contemporary society. They perceived the past as being better, both in terms of their financial status and inter-personal relations (see Tarkowska 2002). The following is a particular reason for this critical opinion: *Before, I had enough to meet the children's needs, nowadays I cannot buy things for them as I do not have enough money*. The respondents perceived their financial status as a drastic deterioration of their living conditions, a degradation of their living standards, and a lack of perspectives for their children and grandchildren. *Instead of having a better life, our living standard keeps deteriorating. Now my life is hard, it is hard to make ends meet* (I/3). They idealised the past, and very often compared their present situation to a previous one, or to the situation that, in their opinion, should be. This comparison definitely made their present situations look worse. In the past, (…) *there was no entertainment as we were poor. But we were happy because we had work, the children went to school, we went to work and then came back. I did not earn much, but it was enough to live on* (H/3). The past was better as they had work and could earn extra money: *When I had little money, I did overtime in the factory, and on Wednesday I received 300 or 280 zloty, and it was enough to buy food to last until the end of the week. And today there is no extra work available to earn extra money. The past was not easy but in a way, it was different* (D/3). Increasing social inequality made them critical: *I cannot accept this injustice, when I hear that salaries paid to those who work in these positions are so high, I realise that they should earn more, but this huge difference is very unfair* (O/3). *And now it is worse, now it is really hard to live, our life is so modest, and we are struggling not to die of starvation* (D/3). The situation was worse because people had no work: *Can you imagine that the guy is forty years old and is unemployed, with three children to maintain, this is incredible. But this is how the system works and this is how it has to be. No one can help* (D/3).

They had a feeling of deep harm and injustice. The unfavourable situation they lived in was beyond their control, and they perceived it as unfair and harmful. *Now I would wish for only one thing, for my grandchildren to reach stability in life, have enough to eat and enough clothes, nothing more. I do not aspire for them to be rich, this is unnecessary. The problem is that nowadays people aspire to be rich and that is why the world is such a bad place* (G/3).

In the biographies of the women of the older generation poverty is present at each stage of their lives. They all experienced poverty during their childhood and old age. Many respondents also experienced it during their adulthood. Family situation, historical events and processes of social and economic transformations have clearly impacted the lives of the women of the older generation. Difficult financial situation in the family of origin, where the small farmland was the main source of income, unemployment or the father's alcoholism, have ultimately led them to the decision of giving up education and starting systematic and paid employment already in the childhood. World War II, hard and multi-year work as Łódź textile workers, successful or in most cases unsuccessful and alcohol-dependant marriage, divorce, sometimes disease or death of the husband, low retirement pension, the feeling of responsibility to support their adult children, who in many cases were unemployed and depended on their support, and the need to care for their grandchildren, represent the main experience of the women of the older generation.

Chapter 3

Poverty in the biographical experience of women from the middle generation – 'mothers'[1]

Women of the middle generation were born in the mid-1950s as part of the post-war *baby boom* generation. Their childhood and adolescence fell in a period of relative *prosperity*, which is also referred to as the period of 'Poland's road to socialism'. Compulsory collectivisation of agriculture was rejected and private land ownership maintained. The craft sector developed and investments were made in the production of consumable goods. Economic plans also addressed housing development and educational infrastructure under the theme 'A thousand schools for the millennium of the Polish State' (Raport Społeczny 2005).

The respondents in this study entered adulthood at the end of the 1970s/early 1980s, when the first signs of the approaching crisis and economic recession, which closed the decade of 'socialist modernisation on credit', were observable. In terms of consumption, living standards decreased, particularly for workers, old-age pensioners and recipients of disability payments. Housing shortages also intensified. 'The secondary circulation of the economy', employment migration, use of external loans, redistribution of income between urban and rural areas, presumption and re-naturalisation of commercial consumption became an antidote to the intensifying deprivation of material needs (Bojar 1991). *Every option for in-house production of food helped to amortise the shortages* (Beskid 1989: 23). The worsening economic conditions contributed to the fact

1 The middle generation of women, herein refered to as the 'mothers' (daughters of the elder generation and mothers of the younger) is represented in this study by women aged 40–45 years. 13 respondents were married, 3 (after the breakdown of their marriages) lived in consensual unions, and 9 were divorced single mothers. Only one of the 'mothers' worked legally, and one wored on the gray market. The other respondents were unemployed and lived on social assistance benefits. They were not entitled to receive unemployment benefit. Most of them completed elementary school, 4 completed secondary school, and 2 had basic vocational education.

that the generation, which was then entering adulthood, was unable to meet needs on their own, despite required self-dependence and economic and housing independence. They lived with their parents and benefited from various types of help from them (Dyczewski 1994).

The formative experiences of women representing the 'mothers' generation are as follows:

1. In their private lives: disintegration of their families due to alcoholism and violence, low quality of their marriages and subsequent breakdown, and single-parenthood,
2. Loss of permanent employment after the introduction of a market economy in Poland,
3. The trajectory of random events (death and sudden illness).

The lives of the respondents of the 'mothers' generation are determined by their biographical experience, which is dominated by emotionally negative experiences of the disorganisation of family life due to the alcoholism of their fathers, and later of their husbands. Their traumatic experiences also include violence, both mental and physical, on the part of their fathers, when they were children, and on the part of their husbands in their adulthood. As children, they witnessed aggression toward their mothers and siblings, and as mothers, violence against their own children. Unhappy marriages, their breakdown and loss of work after the market economy was introduced represent critical points in their lifetimes. But the women of this generation were the first under socialist industrial order to benefit from parental leave and family allowance funding, when their marriages failed. In contrast to their mothers, they applied for divorce if their marriage was unsuccessful and put their and their children's physical and mental safety at risk. The idea of the divorced single mother became a popular phenomenon in their generation. Furthermore, the problem of poverty in their families was not significant, as up until the time of the country's transformation, they had work. Only the loss of employment changed this status and forced them to apply for social assistance. In the initial stages of transformation, the respondents that had stayed on parental leave went back to work for a short time, and were soon made redundant again. The situation of 'mothers' on the labour market changed drastically, and many were no longer able to find employment that would guarantee financial and social security.

There are two groups of respondents, categorised by childhood experience. One is represented by women who came from dysfunctional families, and the other by women who had a relatively normal childhood, but later had their stability affected as a result of private decisions and events in adulthood, as well as the transformations on the labour market.

The respondents whose fathers were drinkers and aggressors were predestined to be 'left behind', as far back as in their childhood. Most of them completed only elementary school, had patchwork-like history of employment because of changing jobs, taking parental leave, and working at ancillary jobs that did not require any vocational qualifications. Subsequently, under the capitalist economic conditions they became redundant. In addition, their fathers' alcoholism was continued by their husbands. They continuously teetered on the edge of poverty, but divorce and loss of employment marked the moment of accelerated slipping into poverty from which one cannot escape.

The second category of respondents enjoyed a relatively good childhood, however poor matrimonial decisions, divorce and loss of work accompanied by traumatic events (death or serious illness) contributed to their financial inefficiency, and this led to their dependence on the welfare and the need for financial support from their mothers. All of the respondents continue to take various actions to survive, such as temporary work, social benefits, and family support, however they are still unable to meet their basic needs.

Morover, the respondents lost a chance to improve their housing conditions during their middle-age, even if their parents had provided them with saving accounts and had collected money for getting a flat. Those of the respondents who had managed to move into panel block apartments were unable to keep them. They were either evicted or returned voluntarily to their previous working-class neighbourhoods (Warzywoda-Kruszyńska 2003a).

These neighbourhoods gradually turned into poverty pockets with very bad housing conditions, however with low rent. At the time the research took place, all of the respondents from the 'mothers' generation lived in Łódź poverty pockets and were registered as welfare recipients. Hence they might be considered to be extremely poor, as social assistance benefits are granted on means-tested basis to people who have low or no income and meet additional criteria (unemployment, chronic illness, parental insufficiency, helplessness, etc.).

1. Childhood

1.1. Childhood in poverty – the father's alcoholism

Five respondents of the 'mothers' generation have traumatic recollections of poverty resulting from their father's alcoholism, and two from their mother's (of a total number of 25 respondents). One of the respondents reports: *My father liked drinking, he had to have vodka to enjoy himself* (Z/1). Another respondent adds: *My life was sad because my father was an alcoholic, it was a life drowned in alcohol. Dad was hardly ever at home, his cronies were always nearby, and if they were not, he went to buy a drink for himself, and drank it all by himself, he used to go to drink in the basement, and later, in the evening, he would crawl back home, he would kick up heavy arguments, and sometimes he would sleep in the basement. We spent holidays without father, no one used to come and visit us at holidays, we were on our own, dad sometimes had breakfast with us, sometimes not, as he had to go, he did not care about the family* (T/1).

Fathers were absent also in terms of their children's emotional needs. They did not show any interest in their problems. *My father was an alcoholic and was not interested in his children's lives, even when we were little he could come to the playground and take other children to a cake shop, ignoring us* (Z/1). *My father took no interest in me, mum raised me single-handed, she was working, and later she sent me to a kindergarten* (T/1). Every-day life spent with a drinking father was lived in an atmosphere of permanent threat, fear, the lack of a feeling of security, noisy arguments and violence: *Father was unbearable, there were arguments, he was going nuts when he got drunk, we knew nothing but swearwords from him and we could not communicate with him* (Z/1). *When my father got drunk, he used to throw things and call us names* (ZP/1). *We were tense all the time* (T/1) a respondent reports, and another one adds: *My brother had the hardest life with him, as father could not stand looking at my brother, and he often beat him when mum was out* (Z/1).

The women who also experienced their mothers alcoholism received little love, security or emotional closeness: *My mum was rather bad-tempered and nervous, she was no good with children. I was her daughter but I cannot say that she cared much. She would call me 'a cow'. When I was going to my First Communion, my godmother cared more than my mum* (U/1). With the father's alcoholism, families were always short of money as the mothers could never count on their husbands' earnings. *Father's wage was quite good, and if he did not spend the money on alcohol and gave it to mum instead, our living standard was good, but when he spent the wage on alcohol, mum's wage was not enough to maintain 5 people. Sometimes I would go to school without a sandwich, and other children had ham sandwiches, they were eating apples, and the children who had money could buy doughnuts. I did not have it and often went hungry to school. Mum could never count on my father to bring money home* (Z/1). *Father spent everything on alcohol, he had temporary work and always spent the money on alcohol, and there were five of us, so it was very hard for mum to make ends meet* (ZL/1). *Mum had only her wage, dad gave her nothing as he spent all the money on alcohol, and that is why it was so hard for my mum* (T/1).

Families where only the mothers were responsible for their maintenance were always short of money, and sometimes went through financial crises. In many cases, they could only afford modest food: *We were very poor, grandma gave us one egg to share, and it would not be possible for my sister and me to get one egg each, our living conditions were very hard and our family was short of money. We were always missing fruit and sweets, always. We were missing them* (J/1). *On weekdays we usually had white borscht, meat was served on Sundays, grandma cooked different types of pasta dishes, but I remember the white borscht most as I did not like it* (H/1). *Mum had to limit everything, she mixed margarine with butter, and on weekdays she would buy bones, she cooked the borscht using only a small piece of sausage* (Z/1). *Mum was buying whatever she could, cold meats too, but not enough, we used to have bread with butter, jam, and honey, and we drank fruit compote as she preserved fruit in jars every year, so we always used to open the jars and had their contents. Meat was served once a week, and there were weeks when we did not have any meat at all* (T/1).

Sometimes there was nothing to eat at home and the children had to secure the funds themselves to buy food: *Once my sister took out old clothes that we were no longer wearing and some old rugs from the wardrobe, we went to sell them as scrap material to buy dry rolls and half a kilo of sugar, and then we had the rolls with the sugar. There were also situations where we had nothing to eat and the neighbours invited us for lunch when mum was at work* (Z/1).

1.2. Education

Women brought up in the families of alcoholics finished their school education earlier, usually at the elementary level (in many cases with the help of the Voluntary Labour Corps[2]). There were various reasons why they did not benefit from the educational opportunities offered by the socialist welfare state:

2 The Voluntary Labour Corps were established in 1958 to complement the education system. The VLC's primary objective was to give young people education through work, as well as to prepare qualified human resources for the needs of the national economy. The VLC recruited young adults and adolescents who dropped out of the school system.

1. Due to insufficient financial means: *I could not afford to continue education. I completed elementary school. There was no one who could pay for school to enable me to continue education. I did not even have money to buy exercise-books, people were helping us. I did not complete this school because I had enough, and I said to myself – no, I will go to work, I will try to make a new life for myself* (T/1).

   I was 16 years old when I started work to earn a living, my brother was a very good pupil too, and he could continue his education at a basic vocational school and then at a secondary technical school, but he also went to work. If our father had not been drinking, there would have been more money (Z/1). *I had to start work early, I had to go to work just after I completed elementary school. I could not afford to continue my education. I was a 16 year old girl and I wanted to have fashionable trousers, I wanted to help my mother, and earn money to become financially independent* (E/1).
2. Low self-esteem: *I had no talent to study and I only completed a basic vocational school, my parents wanted me to become a physician, and mum always used to tell me to study and to become someone, but I was not gifted, and now I am where I am* (M/1).
3. Weak motivation to study or pursue other life aspirations: *I completed elementary school, without any qualifications. I did not continue education. I did not go to school, because when I got into trouble at school, I would play truant. I did not study too hard because I was lazy. In general, I spent eleven years at school, and had to repeat three years. I spent much more time playing truant than studying at school. If you did not study, you would get another unsatisfactory grade* (ZA/1).
4. A lack of inspiration and parental supervision: *Upon completing elementary school, my father did not consent to my further education* (J/1). *Dad was at work and my mum did not check on me. When dad encouraged me, I would get an A, and I could learn a poem by heart* (ZA/1).

   Our parents never motivated us to study. They did not encourage us like parents of some other children, they did not tell us that we had to work and study, they did not verify if we had studied and done our homework. We had to do this ourselves (J/1). *Maybe if my mum had motivated me, but she only used to say, go to work, you will earn money and this will be sufficient for you* (Z/1).

2. Adulthood

2.1. Marriage – low capital at the start

Their choice of life partner was a key factor that determined the further lives of this middle generation of women. The family's financial status and the children's life opportunities depended on, whether the husband and father a decent and hard-working man or whether he abused alcohol. The respondents married in the mid-1970s, at ages ranging from 19 to 25, with their husbands usually 2-4 years older than them. The husbands had usually completed vocational schools and worked as bricklayers and workers. Prior to getting married, they had known each other and dated for a short time – a year or two, or for a longer time – five years. Only some respondents had a traditional engagement ceremony. The women usually met their future husbands at work, or through their friends. Some had known their husbands since they were children, as they were neighbours. *We lived close by and his mum wanted us to meet, so we met* (P/1). *We were very close neighbours, and I used to call my mother-in-law auntie, as our parents were friends* (N/1). The representatives of the 'mothers' generation often married under the pressure of pregnancy: *I had Iza just after we were married because I was already pregnant before we got married, and afterwards I sacrificed myself to the child* (P/1). *We were not dating for a long time, and shortly afterwards we had a daughter and had to get married* (ZB/1). *I was nineteen years old when I got married. I was pregnant and I married my husband* (T/1). *I completed school in June and was already one month pregnant with my partner* (M/1). There was a social norm under which children had to be born in wedlock. Only one respondent overcame this pressure and decided to be a single mother, after a certain period of cohabitation. This is how she explains the motives for her decision: *He wanted us to get married very much, I became pregnant, we lived together for a while, and then Bartosz was born, but this life was so turbulent, to say the least, it was full of entertainment, games, and gambling, and such a life was not for me. I started looking at it differently because the baby was on his way, and I had to start thinking about him and make sure that the child had a decent home. So hell started when I moved out, even the police had to be involved. He was coming here and the police had to force him to leave. The prosecutor issued a strict ban on any visits, and now we are happy. No one has been coming here for seven years, no one pulls out the door, we are no longer afraid that someone will knock at our door at night to interrupt our sleep* (ZF/1).

It seems that at least some of the women knew that their future husbands were alcohol addicts. Despite this knowledge, they still decided to get married, in the light of the pregnancy pressure in particular. *My husband loved alcohol, I knew that he liked to have a drink, but I did not know that he liked to abuse it* (P/1). The fear of becoming a 'unmarried women with a child' was greater than the fear of sharing their lives with a man who abused alcohol. Sometimes they had unrealistic expectations that they would manage to change the husbands' behaviour: *I married my husband feeling pity for him as there were so many alcoholics in his family, and I felt sorry for him. He loved me very much* (I/1). *My parents were shocked when they saw him as I had never liked such people, and all of a sudden I wanted to marry a man like this, and I decided that I would help him, and I sacrificed my life because I thought that if I had married him he would have stopped drinking and meeting with his cronies* (L/1).

Pursuant to the law, the wedding ceremony had to be held at a Registry Office, and then, if the couple wished, at a church. Most of the respondents had church weddings, although in some cases, several months or even years after the civil wedding, sometimes under pressure from their parents: *father wanted us to get married at church* (W/1), or under pressure resulting from circumstances: *There was no way out. We had a civil wedding, however they* [the Church] *did not even want to allow our child to receive First Communion* (T/1). The wedding receptions were held in halls, and followed the traditional pattern of the parents funding and organising them. If the father was a drinker, the couple had a very modest wedding ceremony, and the reception for the closest relatives was held at home: *our wedding was a very modest ceremony held at a Registry Office* (R/1). But its organisation still required a major financial effort. The mother of one of the women recollects that *I incurred a large debt and was taking loans to marry my children off* (ZB/3).

The respondents started their married lives with poor financial security. Only some received help from their parents: *The parents-in-law and parents helped us, my mum gave me armchairs, a table and bedding, later we took out credit for young couples and bought a set of children's furniture and a sofa bed* (P/1). After the wedding they usually used credit for young couples[3]. If the mother of the bride was the only person maintaining the

3 Credit for young couples – was a loan provided for financial security, introduced in 1975 as an institutionalised form of financial aid for young married couples. It was specific-purpose credit designated for the purchase of necessary household equipment. It was binding for 10 years, and the terms for its granting depended on the country's current economic condition. The terms covered certain criteria, used to determine whether the married couple was young, specify the amount, interest rate and repayment deadline, and types of products eligible for purchase using it. Balcerzak-Paradowska B. (1985), *Kredyty dla młodych małżeństw*, Warszawa: IPiSS.

family, the young women did not receive their so-called starting capital, and together with their husbands they had to buy everything themselves, *from the fork, from the plate, from the bed, we had to get it ourselves, and everything we now have is our own* (N/1), using credit and instalment purchases.

A lack of apartments was a key problem for young couples at that time[4]. Surveys carried out among newly-wed Łódź inhabitants in the early 1980s (Warzywoda-Kruszyńska, Krzyszkowski 1990) indicated that only 18% of couples had their own apartments after their wedding. Others lived with their parents or in-laws. A similar situation was observed in the study population (Warzywoda-Kruszyńska 2003a). Cohabitation with parents, and sometimes also with grandparents, was a predominant experience. The *gift of accommodation* in some cases even lasted up to a dozen or so years. It was hard to maintain intimacy in such conditions. *Mum bought us a couch and I slept with my husband in the kitchen, and mum with father in the living room* (Z/1).

Despite the protective activities of the parents who had opened saving accounts for their daughters to collect money for a flat, they could not avoid homelessness (in the sense that they did not have their own apartments). The period of waiting for independent apartments was never-ending, but even in such circumstances, with a little bit of luck, people were able to receive substitute apartments administered by municipality. Some respondents rented flats unofficially, without legal registration of the fact. Housing shortages vere tremendous and getting a flat admin-

4 The housing situation in Poland was characterised by a permanent shortage of apartments in relation to community needs, and was rated the worst in Europe. In the period 1950–1970, the shortage of apartments in relation to needs was estimated at 1.3 m apartments, with 117 households per 100 apartments (Andrzejewski 1973). In 1972, a multi-annual plan of housing development for 1971–1990 was drafted, assuming that 6.6–7.2 m apartments should be built. The plan was actually implemented in 1976–1980. In 1980, the number of available new apartments began to fall systematically (except for 1987) (Założenia 1994). Since 1990, housing has been regulated with the rules of market economy. Terms of financing for housing development have been changed, which has resulted in its drastic reduction (the numbers fell from 190,000 apartments p.a. in the late 1980s, to 65,000 in 1994, due to the fact that new apartments were not affordable to most of the families that had been waiting years for them, as well as the dramatically growing debts of housing cooperatives and the increasing insolvency of some of the families living in cooperative apartments). In November 1994, the following results of an evaluation of Poland's living conditions were made public: 1.5 million households were without apartments, approx. 1 million apartments were completely unsuitable to live in, and some part of the housing resources were insufficiently equipped (Założenia 1994).

istered by municipality was like a miracle. The respondent describes the process of receiving an allocation for a substitute apartment as follows (One day) *a neighbour with whom I had a nodding acquaintance came to my father. He said that finally he had received an apartment in a block of apartments on Wojska Polskiego street. He came to my father to ask him to paint another apartment. So I asked him: 'Sir, dear neighbour, why do you want to renovate that apartment?' 'I need to return the keys* [to municipal housing administration] *because I have received a new apartment'. Jesus Christ! So I told him, 'Please, could you promise me that you will not return the keys before I tell you that it is ok to return them?' And he replied, 'Alright', and just listen what happened then. I told him that I had been registered in a list* [of people who were eligible to receive a substitute apartment].

This respondent had an allocation to receive an apartment in two years' time, however she managed to secure a favourable attitude of a female official, who issued a decision to grant the apartment vacated by the neighbour to the woman. *I got this apartment. Practically it was a one-room apartment, which this gentleman divided into two parts with double-winged doors. There was no toilet, no gas installation, it had a sink, the old type, mounted in a common space corridor. The floor was in a terrible condition, your foot could get stuck between panels, and you could break it* (P/1). Despite that, the woman was happy because her living conditions improved. She had a independent apartment. The people who did not have saving accounts established by parents and therefore could not apply to be registered on the waiting list of municipal housing administration, were looking for other options to obtain substitute apartments (Warzywoda-Kruszyńska 2003a):

1. They damaged the premises in which they had lived to such an extent that staying in them became dangerous: *The apartment was in an awful state* [the walls in the basement were overgrown with fungus and provided a habitat for snails], *that is why later on I was trying to get a different apartment. A committee came, but they did not issue their consent. And in the end I had an idea about the chimney. There was a chimney on the roof, and we knocked the chimney down to make a hole in the roof. When the chimney fell down, a hole formed in the kitchen. I had glasses, and a lamp shade there, and I left everything unchanged to convince them that the damage had not been intentional.* [My husband and brother] *collapsed that roof. The fire brigade came. And I had a small child, so we could not stay without a roof, and only then they granted me this apartment on Wieniawskiego Street.* The apartment in which the woman still lives, *offers no comfort, there is nothing there, neither running water*

nor toilet. You need to go outside. A real disaster in winter, when the water freezes. I feed the stove with old slippers, old clothes, and with a little wood. But finally, there are no snails on the walls (ZB/1),

2. They broke into empty buildings designated for demolition: *They were demolishing that building, so everyone received an apartment, first my brother, then mum, and finally me* (R/1),
3. They broke into premises vacated by former tenants who had received apartments in other blocks. A respondent decided to break into a fourteen square-metre apartment through the attic, *which had holes so big that you could see the world through them, but I simply made this decision as the landlord from whom I rented the apartment* [before] *used to harass me all the time; he liked alcohol and would not leave me alone. I was fed up and said to myself 'That's enough', and I broke into the apartment and then filed an application. I was already living there when I filed the application* [to a housing division to grant a decision on this apartment]. *It took me a year to get this apartment* [i.e. the positive decision on its allocation]. *This is what they told me at the housing division: You are unemployed and you have to find a job. But who would employ me if I did not have a registered residence? It was a vicious circle. I was looking for a job. I was desperately looking for any job, to become employed, without the residence registration. I was wondering when they would come to tell me to move out, to evict me and my little child from the apartment. I was saying, 'Where will I go to live? This will be a disaster without work, without money and an apartment'* (ZF/1). The respondent was lucky. She found a job as a cleaner at a school and received the allocation for the apartment she had wanted to get.
4. They applied for eviction from their parents' apartments (both parties arranged to use such a method): *Mum evicted me as there was no place for me at my mum's. She had a room with a kitchen, and they granted this apartment to me* (Z/1).

Young couples, if they were able to afford this, rented rooms or apartments, usually unofficially, as officially the private housing market did not exist.

2.1.1. The drinking husband's violence and aggression

In the middle generation of women from pockets of poverty, their husbands' alcoholism and the related violence towards the family was an experience that significantly impacted their further lives, and the lives of their children. Eleven out of the twenty five respondents lived in such marriages.[5] Only in some cases the husbands were alcoholics at the start of their married life. Rather, the problem of their drinking intensified with time, which deteriorated the couple's relationship.

Consequently, the families of alcoholics began to manifest dysfunctionalities in terms of child rearing, socialising and emotional aspects. Non-drinking relatives suffered from co-dependency due to the alcohol problem, which led to permanent mental stress. The families' daily lives revolved around activities focused on the alcoholic and his drinking. Gradually, the family consented to incurring the increasing cost of alcohol, which consequently led to psychosomatic disorders, neuroses, emotional problems, and feelings of despair and hopelessness. They released the alcoholic from responsibility for his drinking, and in some cases started drinking with him (Sztander 1995).

Physical and emotional violence is the most traumatic experience resulting from the husbands' alcoholism. The problem of domestic violence towards women and children is a confirmed fact in Poland. It is difficult to identify the precise scale of this phenomenon, however some statistics indicate that 98% of offenders are men, and in terms of victims, wives 81%, mothers 8% and ex-wives 5% (Przemoc w Rodzinie 2000: 35). Studies by the Public Opinion Research Centre in 1993 and 1996 indicate that 18% of married women admitted that they were victims of domestic violence, where 9% were beaten on numerous occasions, and 9% sporadically. On the other hand, 41% of divorced women admitted that they were beaten on many occasions, and 21% sporadically. The survey results also show that 49% of women knew at least one woman beaten by her husband, which implies that many women did not admit to being victims of violence (Przemoc w Rodzinie 2000). The number of cases of domestic violence filed in the country's courts constitutes a fraction of all cases. In a great majority, the victims refused to initiate proceedings against their husbands or decided to take no further action. Despite this finding, the number of men convicted for domestic violence increased, and over 80% of verdicts involved imprisonment that was conditionally suspended (Przemoc w Rodzinie 2000: 33).

This is how one of the women described it: *After six months of marriage, everything started to fall apart, my husband beat me a lot and now I am worn out, he used to hit me in the stomach, and I suffered from nu-*

---

5 Researchers interested in rural areas where state-owned farms had been closed, addressing the problem of alcoholism in communities suffering from permanent poverty (Tarkowska 2000; Perepeczko 2002; Osińska, Śliwińska 1999). A. Golczyńska-Grondas 2004 wrote about the addictions of men from Łódź pockets of poverty.

merous fractures, I had to stay in a hospital, he beat me badly once, then even more badly again, and I was taken to the hospital, he broke my jaw on the third occasion, and even when our community support police officer saw me, he could not stand looking at me as I looked really bad (ZP/1).

I used to go to work with a black eye, or I was very sleepy, and my colleagues were asking me what had happened, so even at work they took interest. When I went to work in such a state they thought that I was drunk and had been partying all night, and I was close to tears as he had beaten me, and they were telling me that I was partying (ZB/1).

Respondents also experienced violence when they were defending their children. *My husband did not care about the children, as if they did not exist, when I got pregnant with the other child he told me to have an abortion as he did not want the other child, I told him that I did not want the abortion and when the son was born he started to be violent to our daughter, it was unbelievable* (M/1).

The drinking and aggressive husbands limited their wives' social contact: *He would not let me out when I wanted to go out, I had to leave through the window, as he was standing there with an axe, and I could not go out. When I went to see my mum and then came back home, the door was locked and I was unable to get inside, I had to call the police, and only they told him to open the door to let me in. He locked the door and I could not get inside* (ZB/1).

In literature (Dobrzyńska-Mesterhazy 1996: 121; Pospiszyl 1994: 193), the problem of women staying for many years in such relationships is explained as:

1. The model of a mental trap – the women feel responsible for the quality and sustainability of the relationship, and fight to maintain it.
2. The model of a situational trap – the women feel that they are in the situation with no way out, and they worry that leaving will result in more losses than benefits.
3. The model of a fear trap – they have an exaggerated and often unrealistically negative perception of themselves as someone who will not be able to manage on their own, and particularly, that they will be unable to secure their children's financial needs.
4. The model of acquired helplessness – an intensifying feeling of helplessness due to the lack of positive results from actions they undertook to improve their unfavourable life situation.
5. Stockholm syndrome – a paradoxical defensive response which manifests itself through sympathy for the aggressor.

The relevant literature indicates a syndrome of specific characteristics of women who experience violence. They financially depend on their husbands, have a low self-esteem and a strongly developed need for dependence. They lack confidence, have a strong feeling of incompetence and identity with the traditional division of roles in the family. They permanently experience stress, the feeling of helplessness, fear, depression and neurosis. All the respondents have these characteristics. *My husband secured a very good financial status, he was resourceful and always had money, but I did not get any warmth from him, I had everything because I had money, but it did not matter as I had no warmth, he drank every day, and unfortunately had affairs all the time, I finally had a nervous breakdown and was unable to go out. My mum had to go with me everywhere as I had the feeling that everyone was staring at me, I was shaking. I had to take medication and have appointments at a private clinic* (M/1).

They demonstrate a strong sense of guilt and responsibility for the husbands' behaviour. They keep blaming themselves: *It was also my fault as when he came back home, they were drinking here, maybe if I had told them to go away at once, but I was scared to speak, so he invited his cronies after work and they were drinking over there, in the kitchen, and I was staying here, in this room, with the children. Maybe if I had told them to go away at once, but I was scared to speak, and anyway, if I had had them leave, he would have beaten me, so they often drank until midnight, or partied until one a.m.* (ZB/1).

The women are ashamed that they experienced violence, and they prefer to hide this fact. They started asking for help only as a last resort: *I did not like to complain to people, I did not ask for help, I never asked for any favours as I was ashamed to admit that my husband was a drinker. I was so ashamed to admit to my colleagues at work, and even my mum did not know about this for a long time. I generally kept it secret* (Q/3). *I filed for divorce because my neighbours helped me, my mum was so busy and I was ashamed to tell her as she already had enough worries. People helped me. Neighbours went to my parents but I was too scared to say anything* (ZP/1).

The respondents took different attitudes towards their husbands' alcoholism and violence. The literature indicates that women defend themselves from violence in many different ways, for instance by attempting to talk to the perpetrators. However, this often leads to further outbursts of anger, and so they learn to be quiet. They make the husbands promise that they would stop being violent or stop drinking, threaten that they would call for the police, file for divorce or leave home. To avoid their aggressors they are hiding, and defend themselves by protecting their bodies. They avoid the husbands by *pretending that they did not exist*, and finally, they return the violence (Pospiszyl 1994, Mellibruda 1997). *Every time we were all also hopeful* – a daughter reports – *as he was always promising that it was the last time, and he apologised. We believed him, but later we were trying to convince* [mother] *to lock him out, however it was not so easy as he could not go to live on the street* (K/2). Mothers concentrated on defending their children. They were trying to protect them from evil treatment by the alcoholic husbands: *Once the husband was drunk, he was aggressive to the children, although they were only children. I told him 'Don't', they need peace of mind. They need to do their homework undisturbed. They must respect their father and father must respect them. This is how I was brought up* (R/1). A daughter recalled: *In the situation when he wanted to smack me, my mum was always getting between us, and sometimes she got hit with a cable as she was protecting me, and she always argued with dad about this. Sometimes she would cry, she would never let him hurt us, she was always a good mum. If she had been like our dad, that would have been the end, simply tragic* (M/2).

The respondents protected themselves and their children from aggressive husbands by fleeing home and calling for the police: *When my husband came back home drunk, he was forcing us to leave, and we were coming back only when he went to work, on the following day in the morning. We spent the night at our aunt's or at mum's* (C/1).

Sometimes the police came and took him, so he did not let off steam on us, he was scared. Once they hit him with a truncheon, and when he came back he went to bed. My mum was strong enough and she never showed that she was scared. If he came back and was still mad, she would call for the police again and they arrived (K/2). *Several times the police came and put him in jail for 24 hours. When he came back he was even more aggressive as he was very angry* (ZB/2). *The police often intervened as it was unbearable. He started to invite his cronies to our home* (C/1). Sometimes they did not receive any assistance. *Militia did not use to get involved in marital problems. When I called them they would tell me to get an axe and fight with him* (ZB/1).

Some women started to fight to save their marriages. A daughter reports: *My mum was such a fighter, she did not give up, and she did everything to keep this marriage, for our sake only, she did her best, she did everything, she loved our father and wanted a normal family for us, she paid for his therapy, took him to the hospital, asked, begged, screamed, blackmailed him, but it did not work. Mum made every effort to get rid of father's companions from our apartment. She tried to discourage him from bringing them home, but as soon as she was out, the drinking companions were arriving. She made the companions leave, so he started bringing them when she was out. She arranged therapy for him at Aleksandrowska* [a psychiatric hospital], *but he gave it up at his own request, and that was the last attempt. After that mum decided to leave him* (K/2).

2.1.2. Taking responsibility for the finances and organization of family life

In families with alcoholic husbands, the entire responsibility for family maintenance fell on the wives. The husbands' earnings were irregular, due to the fact that they either quit their jobs or were dismissed on disciplinary grounds. If they earned some money, they spent it on alcohol, not their family. So it is not surprising that, *basically it was always hard, we lived on mum's wage* (K/2), a daughter of one of the respondents reports. Another adds: *Mother could only rely on the money she earned herself, she could never count on father's money, as he spent it on alcohol* (C/2). Another respondent reported: *My husband never managed to give me any money. He enjoyed drinking so much that he spent all his money on alcohol, then he would spend all money from our family budget, and if he only could, he would take all our property and the money I was hiding so providently from him, and spend it on alcohol* (P/1). The women used different methods to get money from their husbands: *Father would give the money if* [mother] *forced him to. He would give it to her, provided that he was sober, sometimes he even gave her extra money as he simply had to get fed; but it was forced, involved pressure, shouting, it was squeezed out* (K/2) – one daughter reports, and another one adds – *Mum often sent me to go to the factory on payday to prevent him from going out and spending the wages on alcohol* (F/2).

The husband's irresponsibility resulted in 'overloading' of the women's roles as wives and mothers. They had to combine the work which secured income for their families with their family duties. *When I married my husband, I turned into a housewife, I had to carry coal, do laundry and clean the apartment all by myself, my husband never took me out, and I also had to care for his brother as he was single, and there were two children too* (ZP/1). The drinking husband never got involved in childcare. *Dad was going his own way, and mum spent all her spare time on doing laundry, ironing, helping children with learning and checking their homework, I do not remember any situations when she would have free time, she spent it on looking after us instead* (K/2), one daughter recalls.

Mothers changed jobs to try and reconcile family duties with work. Sometimes they had to change their places of employment. Some resigned to reduce their travel time to a minimum, as their workplace was too far from home: *I had two children and I requested the manager to transfer me to another plant by mutual consent to be closer to my children. I wrote an application and it was approved* (T/1). They changed positions within the same company: *I became a cleaner because my child was small and the cleaning job was better for me* (M/1). *After I had children, I started taking cleaning jobs, I had to be at work as early as four (a.m.), I did the cleaning in the morning and could be back at home by half past seven to wake the children up for school* (Z/1). If they had no other options, in emergency situations they took the children to their workplace, or they decided to resign and take a job in a place where they could bring the children: *In the past there were jobs like cleaning at a kindergarten, and* [mother] *was an assistant at a kindergarten where we could stay with her. She did some cleaning at the kindergarten, then some at a school, however later on, when we were big enough to stay at home alone, she went back to work as a seamstress* (K/2).

2.2. The breakdown of a marriage

Infidelity and alcohol abuse represent the most common reasons for divorces in Poland. Studies indicate that over three thirds of Polish society approve of divorce. Over 90% of respondents declared that alcohol addition, beatings and abuse were the key reasons justifying divorce (Kryczka 1999). In the study population almost every other respondent of this generation is divorced. Alcoholism, violence and neglecting duties by the husband gradually led to breakdown of marriage. The respondents decided to file for divorce after 8 to 17 years of married life, and after they had exhausted all other options to improve the situation. Separation initiated by the wife's moving out was an attempt to terminate the unhappy relationship. According to a daughter: *My mum had no money, and when we moved out she did not think to get involved in the* [divorce] *proceeding, she only thought how to buy essential things* (K/2). Sometimes the husband moved out: *I told him to move out as my mental condition was so bad that I did not trust myself and was ready to do anything, I was trying to poison myself because of him, that is what he had done with me, unfortunately, and do you know why? Because I loved him very, very much* (M/1).

Almost all the respondents decided to get divorced due to the men's alcoholism and the violence they had experienced. *Mum filed for divorce as he kept beating her, and finally she surrendered* (ZB/2). *Mum could no longer cope, he was always ready to beat her, we were older then and convinced her to file for divorce. I was 17 years old when mum divorced father* (Z/2). The decision provoked different responses from their families. One respondent experienced complete disapproval: *Father told me that they did not understand me and that I disgraced them* (W/1). Other respondents received help in terms of arranging formal issues: *He tormented me for a long time, and I did not want this, but finally I had a nervous breakdown. Everyone was telling me to get divorced and leave him. So finally I made this decision, I listened to the advice and left him, I got divorced, my brother helped me with the divorce proceedings and wrote a petition* (ZB/1).

The divorce proceedings sometimes took years: *The divorce proceedings went on forever, since 1995, as he either caused delays or claimed that he had no solicitor, or that the solicitor was busy, so the proceedings went on forever, and everything had to be postponed till the next month, it was a rather long process, which took almost 4 years* (C/1). Some cases are still pending: *My husband has not consented to our divorce, it has already taken twelve years as he does not attend the divorce hearings, he simply could not care less, he attended only one hearing* (ZL/1).

2.2.1. Divorce and its consequences

Divorce is classified as an event of critical status (Beisert 1994). A life event receives this status if it is emotionally important to an individual, introduces disorganisation, involves a high risk of losing such key values as self-esteem and love, and results in reduced income and a loss of the feeling of safety. To handle a critical event, the individual needs to undertake new actions to cope with the situation, find new ways to function under conditions of mental strain and imbalance, through subsequent phases: denial, mourning, anger, adaptation (Beisert 1994a). The literature emphasises the bivalent nature of divorce. On the one hand, it can contribute to personal development, through acquisition of new skills and attitudes, and result in a worsening of the financial and emotional situation of the individual on the other. According to Beisert, divorce is a development-stimulating opportunity for both genders. The negative impact of a marriage's breakdown depends more on the coping strategy employed than on the gender of the divorcee. In the process of coping with their divorce, both men and women make mistakes which affect the effectiveness of their actions (Beisert 1995). Assuming all responsibilities for raising the children and maintaining incomplete families was a difficult experience for the women.

In the study population, a divorce that was requested by the women resulted, in many cases, in positive emotional consequences: *I was coping much better soon after my husband left. I started feeling more confident, mentally stable and safer, and my physical condition also improved, I am doing much better now, I am no longer scared when I come home, I used to be scared when I was coming back before, I am happy in my current life, I have rejuvenated a little, I am happy that I am alone with my children, I feel rejuvenated, I was very skinny and did not sleep at night, because we had to escape through the window at night. Now I am calm, I am no longer scared that he will hit me on my head when I am back at home, our life is peaceful now, I can go out whenever I like, and be back whenever I like* (ZB/1). When the drinking, violent father moved out, the children's learning conditions improved, and although they were usually unable to catch up with the school programme, most of them managed to complete elementary school.

Divorce was not the final solution to the problem if the ex-spouses had to share the apartment: *It was a nightmare, my husband lived in the kitchen, and I shared the room with the children, he set the apartment on fire and broke furniture* (ZB/1). *I had to try to get him evicted, so it took me a while. He was occupying one room, and we took the rest as there were 3 rooms and a kitchen in the apartment* (F/2).

Single mothers had problems reconciling their family duties with work: *The younger daughter had bronchitis for two weeks during just one month. My mum still worked at the time, so did my dad, and I had no one to leave this child with, so she was ill for two weeks, I had to work for one week, and then she was ill for another three weeks. I went back to work and he* [a foreman] *gave me such a job that I could not earn much, I used to saw leather, and I was earning a really good salary, but then he told me to make protective gloves and I earned very little, and everyone knew that I was a single mother, so I went to see a supervisor and told him that I was not doing the job I had been qualified for and that he should allow me to work one shift doing the job I had been qualified for, and you know, this was when it all started, I remember it as if it happened today, the foreman told me: you will not win with us anyway, and I became so nervous that I could not bear to stay there, and I quit. Then I went to the Employment Office and got a job as a cleaner in a hotel, but that place was full of drunk men and I got fed up with this and quit again. Then I started to work at the ticket office in a theatre, and also started making clothes at home, and since I did not have the skill, I started to learn it* (A/1).

The fact that the women did not have to worry about uncontrollable spending by alcoholic husbands was undoubtedly an advantage to them and their children, however the loss of employment of the only bread-winner risked pushing the family into poverty and making it dependant on social security and the generosity of their parents.

The literature (Beisert 1995) indicates that the divorced women usually applied two strategies:

- *Entering the trap of double regression*. That is, becoming trapped in the children's world and reassuming the role of their parents' child themselves. This excessive concern for the child reduces emotional tension, however, when reinforced by a feeling of responsibility for the divorce it can lead to preoccupation with the child. On the other hand, expecting assistance from parents is a safety buffer. However, extended support which is also inadequate carries the risk of addiction and loss of independence.
- *Change of life orientation*. The women who decided to invest in themselves, to improve their competences, coped best.

There are no doubts that the respondents did their best to meet their children's needs, however their replies do not prove that they were particularly focused on their children. Maybe this results from the fact that their parents, mothers in particular, were strongly involved in caring for their grandchildren. It should also be stressed that in the case of five of the respondents' children, the grandmothers became their foster families, which indicates that the court decided that these children's mothers were unable to raise them. This decision could have been made on the grounds of mental illness or alcohol addiction, which the respondents did not declare during their interviews.

Neither do the respondents' declarations contain sufficient evidence to show that they attempted to redesign their lives in other ways than by a second marriage or cohabitation. In several cases, the next marriage was also unsuccessful due to the partner's problems with alcohol. However several respondents found happiness in new relationships: *I met a partner, and I was rejuvenated due to this relationship, he helps me a lot, comes to visit me, we have known each other for five years, sometimes he stays at my place, children are happy, they do not frown at him and simply like him, his mum is very ill and he takes care of her, I also visit her to help, to give her a bath, and help with the laundry* (ZB/1).

Another respondent reports: *When I met my companion, maybe I treated it like a remedy, I quickly moved into his apartment, and received a kind of love, I recovered from the past events, and he gave me a lot of warmth, the first one secured me financially, while the life with the other one was hard and poor, but he gave me happiness and love that I had not had before, and I was simply everything to him* (M/1).

2.3. Employment

The respondents entered the labour market in the end of the 1970s/early 1980s. In the 1970s, cities underwent economic development and a dynamic increase in employment. New factories manufacturing knitwear, decorative fabrics and carpets were founded, and the existing ones were modernised. In the late 1970s, Łódź faced a labour force deficit, which resulted from the reduced rate of migration, a great popularity of the recently introduced parental leaves and earlier retirement schemes (Marczyńska-Witczak 1996). However the development of the state-owned investments slowed down significantly already in the early 1980s, and Łódź industry entered the era of recession. The private sector gained importance, and in the late 1970s it employed 2.5% of the employed, and in 1988, 13.5% of the employed (Marczyńska-Witczak 1996: 55). Several respondents started their working life as teenagers. Those women below the legal working age became employed through the Voluntary Labour Corps, or worked as 'runners'. They had no problems with finding jobs, and worked under two- or three-shift system as seamstresses, quality controllers at textile factories, ward attendants at hospitals, and cleaners. They often benefitted from parental leave schemes for mothers with small children, which were introduced in the 1970s. Women were eligible to receive a three-year leave until the child reached the age of four years, and if they had another child during the leave, the leave's maximum duration could reach up to six years. Employers were legally required to grant such leaves at the time preferred by a woman as well as provide her with all employee's rights (insurance, support under the Company Social Fund, etc). If a family had low income, they could claim for parental allowance. At the turn of the 1970s and 80s, parental leaves were very popular in working class families, while white collar female employees, representing the social class of specialists in particular, sporadically used parental leave (Warzywoda-Kruszyńska 1985)

In the 'mothers' generation, the suspension of official employment was a means to increase family income in working class families. Mothers on parental leave were attractive employees for the 'grey economy labour market', which underwent a dynamic development in the 1980s. Performing unregistered work while being on parental leave they kept all the rights resulting from their employee status (i.e. insurance, support under the Company Social Fund and Company Benefit and Loan Fund, etc.), and the employer who employed them 'in the grey economy market' did not have to pay relevant indirect labour cost.

The respondents from this generation had a very diverse total period of employment, ranging from 7 to almost 25 years. These significant differences in employment records result from the fact that their employment was interrupted due to the maternity leaves and wilful resignation from work. Therefore, their employment biography reminds a 'patchwork', and is characterised by the lack of the work ethos. For the women of the 'mothers' generation it was easy to find a job thus they did not feel committed to the workplace. This is how one of the respondents describes her employment history, which seems typical for women with low qualifications: *I went to work as soon as I turned 18. I worked a little here, and a little there, I worked for quite a few companies. Initially I worked for a while in the kitchen at a sport's hall. Then I worked in a laboratory, at Milionowa Street. Then I worked at Pierwsze Zakłady* [the name of one of the factories], *and then, in cotton laboratories; the work in the labs was very hard because I had to carry bales, I had to pull them myself, as it was hard to ask someone* [for help]; *everyone had their work to do, and we could not stop, so it was hard. I had to resign as I could not manage on my own* (ZH/1).

The employment biography of qualified workers employed at factories as spinners, weavers and wrappers was a little different. They usually worked for one company for a longer period, and in the 1980s, after the parental leave, which they usually extended by having the other child, they were coming back to work at the same position at the same company. The situation changed radically after 1990. Their history is inter-related with the history of their employers. Factories were liquidated or had to reduce their size. If the respondents were returning from the parental leaves after the company had been divided into smaller branches, one of the branches usually was obliged to re-employ them. However, since there was no work for them, they were dismissed due to random grounds.

The respondents who had vocational qualifications and commenced their employment under better terms often changed jobs, too. A graduate of a secondary technical school of construction was employed in different institutions, and even tried to establish private business in the 1990s. But during parental leave her vocational qualifications turned out to be outdated.

2.3.1. Loss of employment and its consequences

The loss of regular paid employment is the main experience of women of the middle generation: *I have been unemployed for six years. The sixth year is passing* (ZH/1). Most of them lost jobs in the initial years of the transformation (1991–1993) and have had no regular and legal work since then. Companies which economised their employment, dismissed their employees in the way to avoid payment of group redundancies: *Not a single reprimand, never ever, I used to accept extra work, and the supervisor dismissed me, I just recovered from a long-term illness. They dismissed us individually otherwise I would be eligible to receive compensation, unfortunately I received nothing, as they dismissed us individually* (ZP/1).

New forms of employment (such as temporary or contract employment) were introduced, and these were a novelty to the female workers: *At the last place of my employment I covered for a lady who was on a parental leave, and no one told me about this, I did not know that I was covering for that lady, and a month prior to her return from the parental leave I heard that she was coming back in a month and that I would have to leave, so since I had my pride, I wrote an application to terminate my contract of employment* (ZL/1). The loss of employment put them in a completely new life situation. The methods of coping with daily problems which they had used before, did not work in the completely new reality. They had to elaborate new strategies and introduce changes in their daily activities, since the transformation occurred when they had no savings and investments that could help them to start business activity, which was recommended as alternative employment. They also did not work long enough to receive unemployment benefits or pre-retirement benefits. The social assistance benefit and support provided by their parents (mothers) were their last resorts.

However, most of the respondents took various actions and made efforts to get any type of paid employment. They were very active in searching for work. After they lost the right to receive unemployment benefits, some of them managed to find jobs as cleaners or school janitors. They were often employed based on contracts of mandate or temporary contracts. Most of them had no hope to find a legal employment thus they decided to work without registration, as part of the grey economy. Work in private sewing rooms was a temporary salvation for the respondents who knew how to use sewing machines. Such facilities offered them unregistered home-based work, however these companies were either liquidated or went bankrupt when Deputy Prime Minister Leszek Balcerowicz 'sealed' the Eastern border through which clothes made in the sewing rooms were smuggled to Russia. The women lost work again, and since they had no documented legal employment they were not eligible to receive unemployment benefits. The periods of employment in 'the grey economy' became shorter and increasingly more often intertwined with the periods of living on welfare. It was increasingly harder for them to get employed for the period that would entitle them to receive the unemployment benefit again. In the mid-1990s, the respondents started facing serious problems with getting not only a paid job but also any job based on any contract. The work in the grey economy, without registration, at increasingly unfavourable terms was the only opportunity available to them. Due to this situation, they were unable to work for the period that would entitle them to claim retirement pension: *I did nightshifts at a bakery for 2 weeks, he* [the employer] *did not want to register me, paid me 70 zloty, I went to a social assistance office and showed it to them, and they told me that businessmen were beyond their control, it was hard work, so I quit as he did not insure me, he employed me illegally* (ZP/1). Working in the grey economy provided them with very irregular and increasingly lower income, as the periods of unemployment became increasingly longer, and sometimes lasted 2-3 months. If they did have work, it was exhausting, lasting 10 hours a day: *Well, I work under a piecework scheme. My wage depends on the number of pieces I make. You can say that the income is varied, since if I have to I am sewing day and night and on the following day, therefore the home-based work never ends, however during a 'dead season', it is hard to earn money, my daughter and I have about two hundred zloty to live on, so our situation is really hard, we simply count every penny, I do not go to the social assistance office, I take any available temporary jobs to survive* (X/1).

Under the new economic conditions, the labour market was not very friendly to the respondents, partly because of their age: *I go everywhere to find work, and honestly, there is no work, wherever I go and ask for work, they are saying: how old are you, 42 I reply, and then I hear 'thank you, we have no vacancies, I would like to work but they do not want to employ me because I am too old. Because I am too old* (ZB/1). *You have to be under thirty-five years to get a job in this profession, at my age I can only dream of such a job, I have no hope, no hope at all, to find a job, I am simply too old* (ZL/1). *I keep looking for work, but there is no work. They do not want to employ me because I am too old* (P/1). *When he heard that I was 45 years old he started laughing. It was impossible to get this job, 'Ma'm we need young people'* (ZP/1).

Their health was another major obstacle to finding a job: *The state of my health is so bad that not every company wants to employ me, I am very anaemic, my medical test results are bad and many companies refused to employ me* (F/1).

Many of them had serious health problems: *My son died in the army, the 10th anniversary of his death passed this January, a colleague shot him. And when my son died in the army, my world shuttered, I had a collapse, and my husband had a heart attack, I started losing all my teeth after my son's death, I could simply take them out with hands, it was a nervous breakdown, doctors in the hospital said that all the illnesses simply resulted from a shock and severe stress. Now the job agency granted a decision on disability pension for me because I cannot do any work due to hypertension, cardiac arrhythmia and arthritis, now all these illnesses came out, as well as gynaecological problems, and a doctor, an elderly woman, only came in and checked my pressure, and did nothing else. She wrote that I was capable of working, a sedentary and stress-free job, and that I could carry up to 6 kilograms, so where will I find such a job, this is ridiculous* (ZH/1).

Some respondents were already claiming disability pensions, but lost their eligibility pursuant to the amended legislation: *I was a disability pensioner, but only for two years, and then I lost that status as they decided that I was healthy. And I suffer from epilepsy and this illness eliminates me as an employee, no company wants to hire such candidates* (ZP/1).

Employers did not want to employ them as they had children: *I wanted to work as a cleaner but a man asked me if I had children, and I said I did. Oh dear, in this case I cannot employ you as this would involve sick leaves, and I cannot offer you a job, I would be happy to hire you as you are registered at the district labour office and I would be eligible to claim tax reliefs, however I cannot employ you as you have children and this involves sick leaves* (ZL/1).

The respondents continued their efforts to find jobs, and took part in various courses organised by the Labour Office: *I was trying to get a job, but there is no work, I keep asking and searching for this work, however there are no jobs for graduates of the first course for social carers, I was also trained at a job agency, so I completed another course and still did not find a job and they told me that I would not find a job anyway. Do you want to know why there is no work? Employers hire disability and old-age pensioners as they do not have to pay insurance for them, and the government does not care what we are going to live on. I have completed this course to be able to earn my living, but unfortunately whichever company I approached they told me they did not want to hire me, I do not know what I should do next, I have lost all my hope. I completed the courses because I thought that upon their completion I could at least find a job as a ward maid, and now there is no hope for me to find any work, even though I completed the training* (ZP/1). *I enrolled to courses organised by the Employment Department on several occasions, however they never had enough candidates so I never attended the course. They were either too few candidates or I was not accepted because I have children and the training was held during the hours that did not suit me* (ZL/1).

The loss of regular employment lead to a significant reduction – or even the complete loss of income necessary to live on. The women fell into a debt spiral (see Palska 2000), getting seriously behind with payment of their bills: *I fall behind with electricity bills and rent, I have some debts and I would really like to go to work to change this situation. My mum cannot help me as she does not have enough money herself, I do not have a father, nor close relatives, there is only my mum* (ZB/1). Some of the respondents were evicted from their apartments, while others exchanged their apartments for smaller ones, and obtained a lump sum for this transaction: *I had no money to pay my bills, debts reached the amount of three thousand and six hundred zloty, including interest rate, and two thousand and four hundred zloty plus one thousand and two hundred zloty interest rate represented another debt, so I started looking for an option of apartment exchange. I was thinking that instead of eviction I should exchange the apartment, and I did, into the apartment with two rooms and a kitchen, one room for my daughter and the other for me and my husband. Soon I will receive a gas bill and I do not know how I will pay it, I have not paid for water since June, you can pay either every six months or every month, but anyway, I do not know how to pay for this, I am trying to pay for electricity, otherwise they will come and disconnect us, our television set broke down and we have no television set, that's our life. We are terribly poor, the washing machine broke down and I have no money to have it repaired, I wash everything by hand, this is our life, a vegetation after 25 years of work* (ZH/1).

Some respondents had to move out of their apartments in the panel apartments blocks for which they had waited a very long time, to old tenement houses in a pocket of poverty, but were unable to keep these apartments either: *I cannot afford heating, so it is disconnected. Electricians came and disconnected us from the heating system as we did not have money to pay the bills. But we have a coal stove, beautiful, very nice, brown (they have nothing to fuel the stove), I am having dreadful financial problems* (N/1). Other respondents worried that the prolonged period of limited options for paying accommodation-related expenses would finally result in losing their apartments.

The relevant literature emphasises that the loss of work is an event that can lead to a crisis, as it results in strong tension that affects normal functioning. An individual who becomes unemployed loses not only the possibility of earning for living, but also their *psychological wellbeing. The unemployment is a type of a specific psychological dislocation, which dislocates an individual from the conditions in which he or she felt rooted, and which the individual coped in a better or worse way – but always coped, to a new reality deprived of important reference points* (Skarżyńska 1992: 17). The longer one stays unemployed, the deeper his/her psychological discomfort is, and the more vulnerable he/she becomes to stress, depression disorders, fear and concern for the future, helplessness, feeling of ineffectiveness in terms of efforts made to find a job. Consequently this is followed by apathy, helplessness and decreased activity in searching for work, a changed attitude to employment, aggression, alcoholism and even suicidal behaviour. Gradually the unemployed person assumes the attitude of resignation, suffers from emotional breakdown, experiences the feeling of helplessness, hopelessness and disorganisation of social and family functions. It particularly affects individuals that have developed sufficiently strong protective mechanisms and the skill of handling difficult situations, and who receive no assistance and support from others. The lack of assistance is a key reason for the psychological crisis. The long-term unemployment is an experience that can alter self-perception of the unemployed (Bańka 1992).

The loss of work was a psychological burden to the respondents and lead to their severe frustration. Ineffectiveness and inefficiency of their actions induced the feeling of helplessness, hopelessness and pessimism. Discouraged by the failures, the women reduced their efforts to find work, lost their self-confidence and the feeling of efficiency of their actions: *I do not feel like doing anything, I am so depressed that I do not feel like doing anything at all, I can stay at home for weeks, I only listen to the radio and read newspaper ads. I buy the papers only once a week as I cannot afford to buy them every day, so I can only hear job ads on the radio, and if I hear one,*

I make a call. This is completely useless. When I call the potential employers, I realise that many of them are cheats. I go to private businessmen and ask them for a home-based work, I also call the radio station to advertise my availability to do some home-based work, but there is no such work. I cannot see any future, any hope, I just live from one day to another, I worry about food for today and for tomorrow, and I am not concerned about the future. I am 51 years old but feel as if I was 70 (BC/1). They are also more likely to suffer from depression. One mother reported that: *My daughter* [50 years of age] *could not find a job for a long time, she looks unwell, very unwell, and she is so nervous, she was made redundant when the company downsized its employment, she completed a school of hosiery production, and then she was made redundant and had problems with finding work, that is why she approached the community centre and she simply does a cleaning job there. She cannot accept that she is a cleaner, she has two children, her neurosis is so severe that I cannot recognise her, she is screaming a lot and have become so chaotic, I do not know what will happen next, she is ill, I can see that she suffers from neurotic disorders* (ZG/3).

According to Renata Walczak (2000) unemployment contributes to almost complete transformation of self-image. Women who experience unemployment bear the following characteristics: a reduced level of self-acceptance, the lack of effectiveness of their actions, tendency to isolate from the rest of the world, life dissatisfaction and a reduced resistance to stress, a small need for independence from others, a stronger need to express the feeling of inferiority which is manifested through self-criticism, the feeling of guilt or social incapability, a greater tendency to get isolated from the rest of the world and withdrawal from interpersonal contacts. They lack self-confidence and enterprise to fulfil their life goals. They are fearful, have problems to determine their life goals and doubt their potential. The women limit their social contacts with colleagues from work and the financial problems induce the feeling of social isolation in them.

2.4. Health problems and sudden illness as poverty driver and maintainer

Key critical events that forced the women of the 'mothers' generation into poverty included health problems, and particularly sudden outbreak of a serious, chronic and somatic illness, and sudden disability, which lead to a continuous deterioration of their health. Such illnesses as tumours, multiple sclerosis and serious psychological disorders required that other relatives had to provide the women with permanent care and contributed to major financial problems resulting from the need for longer stays at hospital, high cost of treatment and purchase of expensive medication. The poverty started in unexpected circumstances caused by a serious illness, as it forced them to give up their professional activity and become disability pensioners. Even if their previous financial status was reasonable as the husband managed to maintain the family, in the situation of the illness, their financial stability was affected: *I had to sell the car and all my gold jewellery, I lost everything, all my savings, when I had to stay in the hospital for the amputation. My legs failed, the main popliteal artery became blocked and they inserted a by-pass, but my body rejected the by-pass and the leg had to be amputated in 1992. After half a year I went into a hepatic encephalopathy and had to stay in a hospital again and to buy a vaccine again: I was in a coma for ten days and stayed at the hospital, and there were times that I had to spend a lot of money for medication, I had to take a drug for my liver that cost two hundred zloty per package, and it only lasted for a month, I also took drugs for cardiovascular disorders and I had to pay 100% price, and I cannot interrupt this drug therapy* (Z/1). This is how the respondent's daughter recollects this situation: *Dad sold everything then, everything, but it did not help and she had the leg amputated. I remember that we were in a crisis, but grandma helped us, we had food, but our properties were gone, we had to sell everything and each salary of my dad was spent on hospital, medication, everything for mum* (Z/2). Another respondent had a road accident and had to have several surgeries: *A car hit me on a pedestrian crossing, I was crossing the street on a green light, that was a Volvo with a trailer, and it hit me, he should have stopped, and I fell on the road and now have a haematoma in my brain, I need help as I even cannot bend down properly, if I do, I start having vertigo* (T/1).

Outbreak of a serious and long-term illness significantly deteriorated the situation as the women had to suspend their professional activity and became disability pensioners: *My life was very good, but in 1978 a tragedy stroke as I lost my sight, and since 1978 I have been qualified as a pensioner under the second category of disabilities. Walking is difficult for me as I was diagnosed with multiple sclerosis, and now I cannot walk, my legs become stiff and painful, the same with my knees and ankles, and I cannot walk, I suffer from hypertension, have problems with my head and heart and now they have referred me to a cardiologist, I am so weak, it is probably this multiple sclerosis, I have no energy and am unable to do anything, I cannot stand up, I hardly cope and sometimes I have problems with going downstairs* (ZG/1). Another respondent, who lost sight after a brain tumour surgery, was also forced into a dramatic situation by the illness. She lost all her income and depended on permanent maintenance and systematic care provided by her family. She only received a small carer's allowance. She did not qualify for disability pension because of insufficient employment record.

Giving birth to a disabled child was another event that contributed to the women's difficult situation. Such circumstances also forced women to terminate their professional activity, however in some cases the benefit for the disabled child was the only source of income for the whole family.

Poverty in the biographical experience of the women of the middle generation is present during the consecutive stages of their biographies. Not all the women experienced it during the childhood, however each respondent experienced poverty during the adulthood. Difficult financial situation in the families of origin caused by alcoholism of one or both parents, unsuccessful and early terminated education due to the lack of their parents' support in the learning process, early commencement of employment, unsuccessful and alcohol-dependant marriage, serious disease, which led to their unemployment, in some cases death of the husband, and primarily the loss of regular work have contributed to the women's of the middle generation permanent unemployment, poverty and dependence on the social assistance institutions.

Chapter 4

Poverty in the biographical experience of women from the young generation – 'daughters'[1]

Women from the 'daughters' generation were born in the second half of the 1970s and in the early 1980s. Their early childhood coincided with the period of gradually aggravating economic and political crisis of the system of centrally planned economy, when the socio-political transformation was under way. The world, in which they started to consciously participate, was already based on capitalist social order where joblessness was not an exception but a rule in milieus they grew up in.

Their biographies reveal a significant change of social behaviours concerning family formation. The norm of a childbirth within marriage noticeably weakened and motherhood of an unmarried woman was no

1 The young generation – 'daughters' (daughters of the women from the middle generation and granddaughters of the women from the oldest generation) – is represented by 16 women aged 19-25. They had different marital status. Five of them were married and one out of five was childless. Two of them lived in a non-marital relationships with the fathers of their children. Three of them were single mothers who had never been married. One of the interviewees was divorced and raised her children alone. Five women have never been married and were childless. Among the 'daughters', ten women were mothers: 6 of them had one child, 3 of them had two children and 1 of them had four children. The children are were from six months to nine years old. The interviewed women gave birth to their first child at the age of 16–19, immediately after graduation from primary or vocational school. Pregnancies were unplanned. Only one of the young women was legally employed and one of them worked occasionally in the grey market at the time the reasearch was done. Welfare benefits were the source of maintenance for the 'daughters'. Other sources of income included husband's remuneration or support provided by women's or their partners' families of origin. Half of the women have never had gainful employment. Some of them had worked for a short time before giving birth to a child. They had a low level of education. Nine women had primary education, five women had basic vocational education and two of them had general secondary education.

longer something extraordinary. Poorly educated, living in devastated and impoverished neighbourhoods, the girls did not have a chance to find 'high quality' partners. Unlike women from the middle generation, they not always agreed to marry their partners and often chose single parenthood. It cannot be ruled out that single motherhood became related to restrictive anti-abortion law which does not allow abortion upon a woman's request. It may also be related to the internalized norm 'not to kill an unborn child' disseminated by the Church.

Early procreation prevented the women from prior work undertaking, which resulted in their financial dependence on welfare and on generosity of their grandmothers and, more rarely, their mothers. However, the respondents did not treat this situation as particularly discomforting. They rather seemed to treat it as a natural order of things. They represent the first generation of women in our study for whom attributes of adulthood: work commencement and starting a family of procreation are set apart.

Formative biographical experiences of the generation of the 'daughters' which lead to poverty and dependence are related to:

1) disorganisation of life in families of origin,
2) early termination of education and joblessness,
3) early, unplanned motherhood.

1. Childhood

1.1. In the shadow of alcoholism

Childhood of the majority of the studied young women is marked with the experience of violence and disorganisation of family life as a consequence of alcohol abuse by one parent or both parents. Most frequently, the problem affected a father or a stepfather but it happened that both parents were addicted to alcohol. The problem was described by the interviewees as follows: *My parents can drink a lot. They did a lot of harm to me and my siblings. They are drinking and that's it, there is no other way out, you won't persuade them. They don't drink round the clock all the time. They do for a week, then they have a longer break, let's say a few months, and then the story repeats itself and round and round it goes for all these years. I used to love and I still love my father more, since my mom, she is not really important to me, I'm more for my dad. Were it not for my mom* [*who is addicted to alcohol*], *had I been with my father alone, I would have had a better life than with my mother. She cared almost about nothing. This was my father who introduced some discipline, when it was alright and he wasn't on the booze, then he in fact took care of the entire family. Were it not for my mom, everything would be alright. But it is my mom who is at fault. He actually may be doing this* [drinking] *because he sees that my mom is down and he claims that when he drinks he forgets about everything, all of these worries* (ZA/2).

However, the interviewees more often speak of their fathers being addicted to alcohol: *He* [father] *didn't drink all the time, since there were 3 months of sobriety and 3 weeks of drinking, and it was like this over and over again. He could drink for 3 or 4 weeks nonstop, and then there was delirium tremens and epileptic seizures* (K/2). The interviewees were beaten as children and they experienced other forms of violence. Literature on the subject outlines that violence brings about numerous negative consequences in terms of psycho-social and emotional development of a child. It evokes the feeling of emotional detachment, the sense of injustice and loneliness, unsatisfied need for security, blocked need for self-acceptance, low self-esteem, a belief that one is not able to achieve success in any field, emotional lability, inability to enter interpersonal relationships, proneness to depression and isolation (Jundził 1993, Pospiszyl 1994). Neurotic disorders such as night terror, nocturnal enuresis, hyperactivity and low self-esteem are consequences of experiences related to alcohol addiction. The interviewees tell about the lack of love, acceptance and the lack of support usually on behalf of father who is the one who abuses alcohol. Fathers had a devastating impact on their school career, emotional and intellectual development. Neglect appears to be a common feeling: *I don't remember anything that would make me have a positive attitude towards him* [father], *we've never managed to get along. Perhaps he said a few words too many which I'll never forget, since I was 10 or 12 and he would call me terrible names. We didn't talk a lot and whenever we talked we quarrelled, that was usually a heavy fight. He was never really interested in whether I had anything to eat or wear, or whether I was in good health. I remember that when I had exams to secondary school and I came home he didn't ask me whether I passed or not and he didn't even look up from his crossword puzzles. He wouldn't hug me or advise anything or guide me ever in my life. Never in his entire life would he go to parent-teacher meetings, he never knew what my grades were, he would never even look into our notebooks, he would never ask whether we did our homework. All in all, he wouldn't actually be interested in anything. This is what our relationship looked like more or less* (K/2). Another interviewee is telling us: *My childhood wasn't too happy because of my stepfather. Of course, my mom tried to give me as much love as she could. I can't deny that. She would often hug me. But my stepfather was very strict. He had been good to me until my sister was born.*

Then he started to reject me. Only his daughters mattered. I was the last one in a row. I would never deserve anything. When he bought something he would buy it only for sisters, not for me (F/2). They experienced physical violence when defending their battered mothers: *He* [father] *was an alcoholic. When he drank he would abuse us, especially my mom. He would beat her. As the eldest daughter, I've always loved my mom and I love her and I would defend her and that's why I would also often get hit* (F/2). Father's drinking resulted in learning difficulties, which led to early termination of education, placement in residential care or school for children with special educational needs. *When I went to school, I didn't have decent life, for my father would always interfere in my homework when he was drunk. It was so bad that when my mom was absent and if I wrote something wrong, he would hit me on the head. It was a disaster when he was beating me on the head* (T/2). *When I was about to finish primary school, I was sent to residential care because of my parents. I collapsed mentally and physically there. I was crying every day, day in and day out, because I wanted to go home, although this home was rather disgusting. Still, I preferred to be home than in that institution* (ZA/2). At school, the interviewees came across numerous difficulties. They had serious learning difficulties. School was associated with unpleasant feelings from the very beginning of educational career. They had to repeat classes because of failing grades. Some of the interviewees couldn't pass a year two or three times also because of absenteeism. Fights at home meant that they could not study in peace. Being unprepared for lessons, they became an object of ridicule for schoolmates and teachers. They often changed schools when teachers did not want to or did not know how to help them or else when they were moved to grandparents for a certain time. They had few friends at school, one or maximum two who usually were in the same life situation. One of the interviewees recalls: *I was playing with one friend all the time, I wouldn't play with anyone else, I didn't have any other friends* (E/2).

The interviewees managed to graduate from primary school with difficulties, usually aged 17–18. Even if they made an attempt to obtain vocational qualifications, this ended in failure due to the lack of motivation, perseverance and other competitive advantages: *I wanted to be a seamstress. I had sort of internship. This was before wedding. We were dating and I didn't want to go there but only to his* [her future husband's] *place. I would always be sitting at his place. My mom knew nothing about it* (ZB/2).

Although they lived in a modest way, the interviewees agree that they did not experience malnutrition or starvation during childhood: *It was always hard but they got on somehow. I can't say that we had nothing to eat, whether they were drinking or not, there was always something to eat, we were not untidy, although this was rather me who took care of it, since who would do it when your parents are in a daze* (ZA/2).

All in all, there was always something to eat at home (F/2). *As I recall, it was definitely not a disaster but we didn't have enough to provide for everything. There was no hunger ever but we didn't have superb things either. But I don't remember it being very bad. We could afford food. For sure, we weren't dressed up in nicer clothes, we didn't have electric equipment but there was food. We always had lunch, some soup on a daily basis and two courses on Saturday and Sunday, this was always there* (K/2).

1.2. At the grandparents' place

Nearly all the interviewees (except for K/2) were sent to grandparents to save them from violence. Grandmothers (sometimes with grandfathers) formally or informally served as foster families. Grandparents played a special role in biographical experience of the women from the young generation. Almost all of the women of the 'daughters' generation had a strong emotional bond with their grandmothers. Often the only warm words in their statements were addressed exclusively to their grandmothers: *My grandma is such a person that I love her very much, I sacrifice everything for her. If it was not for her, I don't know how it would all come out. She taught me everything in fact and she gave me, I don't know how to put it, such wisdom that she has* (ZA/2). *Frankly speaking, my grandma is the only person that I love very much. She meant everything to me* (M/2). This strong emotional bond resulted from the fact that early childhood of the interviewed young women was actually spent at their grandparents' home. The girls stayed at their grandparents' place to get protection against aggression of their fathers and stepfathers but also to give way to younger kids in their family of origin when their mothers got married again and gave birth to another children. Placement of children at their grandparents' home was the basic form of protection against ill-treatment, aggression and violence of a drinking father who was an alcohol addict. As stated by he mother of one respondents: *My daughter had stayed with my mom for three years I guess before she went to the kindergarten, since my husband beat her, she would be wetting herself because of her nerves, then she was treated in hospital. He would simply often call her names, I would be quarrelling with him, so he would hit me because of her when I was defending her. Nothing could be done and my mom took her* (M/1). Young women most often arrived at their grandparents' place when they were, at the age of 7–8, when they needed a peaceful place to learn. They usually stayed at their grandparents' place for several years.

The girls return home when their mothers decided to leave their fathers. However, grandparents also turned out to be indispensable when a mother reconstructed a family and a stepfather or a mother's new partner did not accept a child from the previous marriage and mistreated the child: *My* [step] *father didn't treat my mom well. He believed that since he worked it was everything. When he drank and even when he didn't drink he would lace into me, so my grandma took me. When I was little I mostly spent time at my grandma's. They took care of me so that my dad didn't beat me. He would always keep an eye on me and I would always get owned for nothing, or something. He treated my brother better, since he was his son, more his blood as he would explain it. With me, he would always push me around and push me and shout at me. He was unkind, my* [step] *father* (M/2). The girls were at grandparents' from the moment of birth when both parents were alcohol addicts. A twenty-one-year-old woman from such a family recalls: *Well, I didn't exactly have a happy childhood. My dad was in prison. Well, and my mom didn't exactly take care of me as she should have. Thus, my grandma took me and she was raising me until I was six. When I was born it happened so that my grandma worked at the same hospital where I was born and she had connections there. She learned when we were supposed to leave the hospital and she took me immediately. Then my mom took me and so I lived with my parents until I turned 18* (ZA/2).

1.3. Mother's divorce. Breaking off relations with the father

Parents' divorce did not stick in daughters' memory if it took place when the girls were small. Since fathers did not seek contacts with them, the interviewees had little to say about them. They were not aware of father's place of birth, education, current situation or place of work. All ties with the father were broken when he left. Only a few of the interviewees had contacts with their fathers shortly after their parents' divorce. In a few cases they would visit father's parents once a year during vacations. Fathers rarely made any material contributions: *I remember that he took me to the store once and bought me shoes, a rucksack, he bought me a doll. On the whole, he didn't buy me gifts* (A/2). The young women whose mothers divorced their husbands after a dozen of years in a relationship did not maintain contacts with their fathers out of their own volition. As teenagers, they were happy that their fathers were no longer at home. All of them believed that the decision about the divorce was the right one. Fathers turned into strangers: *Frankly speaking, we didn't see each other for 8 years, as long as we don't live together. I see him in the street sometimes but we never talk to each other. It is as if my father doesn't exist, it doesn't hurt. My mother didn't pit us against our father. She would even make sure that we made a congratulatory scroll on Father's Day. She would never tell us which one of them was better. She wouldn't judge my father, she would never drive a wedge between us. She didn't forbid us to visit our father after he had left. She only didn't want him to visit us* (K/2). Ties with father's family were severed, too: *They told my sister that since our father divorced our mother, we had no business there, since this was no longer our family, we were excluded from that other family* (ZB/2).

2. Adulthood

2.1. Early, unplanned motherhood

Unplanned, early motherhood which results in termination of education plays a critical role in the interviewed young women's life experience. *I got pregnant with my first child and I didn't go to school any more, as there was no way to. I gave birth to a child, I had to be at home and take care of a baby. There was no way I could go back to school and graduate from it. I gave birth to the second child two years later and this was the end of my schooling. I don't regret I have children* – she adds – *it seems to me that it is better to have children rather than not. But the thing is, I was young and I wasted school and young years of my life* (M/2). Motivation for early partner relations was often the wish to 'escape' from home where they experience alcohol abuse, conflicts and no emotional bonds. They searched for the feeling of security and cordiality in their own partner relations. In such cases, the interviewees have known their partners for a short time. Early motherhood was a consequence of unplanned pregnancy, most often so-called surprise pregnancy. The interviewees became mothers as early as at the age of 16–17. They gave birth to their children immediately after graduation from the last grade of primary school. *I was already pregnant at the end of the 8th grade and I was getting married in June* (B/2). Some of them had to take their final exams on an individual basis.

They got pregnant with accidentally met men whom they had known for a short time or sometimes for two or three months: *My brother brought a colleague along and it all started. It was surprise pregnancy, I was 19 and I was already pregnant. Then my boyfriend got behind bars… He spend three years in prison and he was released in 1998* (E/2). Young women's partners were men with low, primary or basic vocational education. They came from incomplete families. They lived with their mothers and were dependent on them. They worked occasionally or were jobless. The young mothers did not want to formalise their relationships since their partners grew up in families with problems of alcohol addiction or criminality. Some young men themselves abused alcohol, half of them were criminals. These men usually had no permanent employment and usually worked occasionally on construction sites, if they worked at all. After delivery, the interviewees maintained no contacts with the fathers of their children. These contacts ended often before the child was born. The young fathers showed no interest in their children. *He doesn't maintain any contact, but I was trying to establish paternity. He doesn't visit his child until now* (M/2). The women did not want their children to have contacts with them.

Whether and to what extent single motherhood pushed the respondents into poverty depends to a large extent on the attitude of young women's parents to their early pregnancy: *My dad was infuriated and he wouldn't speak to me. My mom would talk to me all the time. She was crying in the beginning for she was awfully surprised since I didn't have bad company, I would never go to any discos, I was a homebody. And there is such a shock here, I'm pregnant. How did it happen that I was pregnant, I always used to be this little Cathy, so innocent. My mom cried in the beginning and she was outraged but then she would behave normally in relation to me* (M/2). Her father decided that his daughter would have to provide for herself: *They've decided that it would be best if I lived by myself and they moved me here and I was all by myself. My grandma helped me a bit, she helped me to arrange things. My dad wouldn't help me, he didn't stay in touch with me. And he visited me on his own initiative just before the childbirth and we embarked on a conversation* (M/2).

The women whose parents helped them were in a better situation. *I told my dad that I was pregnant and my dad told me that there was nothing to worry about, that we would cope with it* (E/2). *I was afraid to tell my mom but somehow* [father] *gradually, gradually made her ready for it and she said – well, ho-hum* (B/2).

Five young women legalised their relationships with their children fathers while being pregnant. Their husbands were peers from the neighbourhood. They got acquainted with via friends and have known each other for quite a long period – two or three years. All married couples had both civil and church wedding. Except for one of the married couples, the organization of the wedding and the wedding party was financed by parents of both spouses. Grandmothers assisted them financially, too. In one case parents of the groom refused financing the wedding party since they disapproved the marital decision of their son. *My boyfriend organ-*

ised the wedding himself and my parents gave him the money back later on, after the wedding (B/2). The decision about getting married was met with disapproval because of the young age of the girl and her low level of education. *My parents-in-law occupy a high position, they are well-educated and my parents are not. They wouldn't agree to the marriage because I was young and was not educated. I had problems with them before the wedding but now everything is fine, we get along somehow* (B/2).

One of the married women – a mother of two children – was already divorced at the time of the research because of her husband's alcohol addiction. Three young women decided to live in an informal relationship with the fathers of their children but planned to legalise their relationship in the nearest future: *We intend to get married on Christmas if we have money for it. This is what we have to start with. But we do intend to. I'm saving money on the building society book* (E/2). *We're not married since these are hard times but baptism is planned for March and we're planning to get married. But only a civil wedding is planned since it's more important than the church one.* (ZA/2).

2.2. Being a mother

The young women were happy they were mothers although they were conscious of the consequences of this situation: *I love my child, I'm happy that I have a wonderful child* [however] *I would advise young girls who are 19 years old or so not to have children, get married because it is really hard. These young women, they should think it over. I didn't think it over, I wanted to have my own family really badly and I wanted to have my own flat, to feel I was in charge of my life. And now, what am I left with? I wanted to tell young girls they shouldn't hurry into getting married and having a child* (ZB/2). *I do my best* – another woman says – *so that my children have different childhood than I had, since I witnessed fights, I was pushed around. I'm extremely happy there are no fights they would be witnessing, there is no alcohol addiction they would be witnessing, there is peace and calm and this is the most important* (M/2).

The young women spared no effort to meet the needs of their children: *I buy high-quality cold cuts only for children* (Z/2). *As soon as I get the money, the first thing I do is to go and buy food for children so that they always have food in the fridge* (M/2). They would buy sweets for children only, purchase better food, cottage cheese, yogurt for them. *It happens that you would eat something of worse quality but you would buy a different cold cut, pork or poultry ham for your child, you would leave something better for them* (F/2).

2.3. Outside the labour market

Among the studied population, only two women had had steady employment. One of them gave up work out of fear that her husband – an alcoholic would remove all the things out of her flat during her absence. The other one was dismissed as part of redundancy having returned after her childcare leave. The former one was childless while the other one provided for two sons. The latter was constantly working in the 'grey market'. She did not have a permanent employment contract. She accept it because: *The situation looks this way, there is no way out. You have to manage somehow in order to have a job and earn the money somehow* (F/2). Half of the interviewees of the 'mothers' generation were never been employed. Having finished primary school while already being pregnant, the young women had no vocational experience. After the childbirth, two of them undertook occasional work because of the difficult material situation. However, they worked for a very short period of time, barely for a few weeks and they gave up their jobs due to a poor health of a child and the lacking childcare opportunities. *I couldn't* [work], *he* [son] *is of feeble health, and my husband yells at him, I told him already that he was too little, he didn't understand, I can't leave the baby with my husband* (ZB/2). In order to get a job they concealed the fact that they were pregnant: *I had to hide the fact that I was pregnant as soon as I got pregnant, since they wouldn't hire me. I had to take up a job in order to buy what was needed for a baby. I had to buy things which were necessary, since my boyfriend* [child's father] *was still in prison. Hence, I hide the fact I was pregnant until the third month of pregnancy* (E/2). Those who got any employment were subjected to exploitation: *I was exploited by my boss. He registered me as an intern while I would be working full time. I was in fact in office for 8 hours and, above all..., And the money I got per month was a pittance... I resigned after all because there was no sense to work for such a pittance* (Z/2). To get welfare benefit for themselves, mothers had to register in the Employment Agency and accept one of three job offers. *When my baby was over six months, they* [the Employment Agency] *sent me to work. They gave me a job, so I went there. However, they* [employer] *didn't want me because my baby was too small.... So they gave me another job. I went there and they wanted to employ me but it was too far away and there was no one to take care of my baby. My mom is sick and I'm afraid to leave my child with her even now since she can get a fit* [of epilepsy] *any moment,* (E/2). *The truth is that nobody wants to take me on since I have a small baby. This is what this is all about. I would have someone to take care of the baby since my mom could do it but they simply don't want to. The baby is simply too small, I learned that* (D/2). Some of them did not even try to find a job since no one can replace them in their family duties: *What am I supposed to do with two of my children? I can't leave them by themselves. I wanted to go to work. Damian started school, I have to bring him to school and bring him back from school. And what about the second child? No one will give me a job at hours that suit me. Besides, my son is sick. He suffers from hepatitis B. He is vaccinated. I have problems with him. I have to go to hospital and I have to visit doctors every now and then* (M/2).

The interviewees who were raising their small children put off the job search until the moment when their children would reach kindergarten or school age. All of them wanted to undertake employment when having raised their children. However, having no experience in the labour market, they had no idea what kind of job they would like to have. All of them planed to work 'somewhere'. They were unable to say what they would like to do in the future. Some of them absolutely did not care what kind of job it would be since it was only important for them 'to earn money'. The majority of them had no educational plans and they did not intend to continue learning. As one of them stated: *I'm extremely happy I've just graduated, exams are over* (D/2). Only one of the interviewees seemed to realise she could have better employment prospects thanks to education and she intended to study at an evening high school when her children are older.

2.4. Dependency on family support and social welfare

Most of the interviewees from the young generation were economically dependent on their relatives and welfare. Only one married woman claimed that her family of procreation were financially and materially self-sufficient. Her husband worked on a construction site for a private company. He used to be a tailor's cutter but resigned from that job because of low income. This couple was supported by their parents at the beginning of their married life (they provided the young couple with a flat, furniture and household appliances) and was able to provide for themselves thanks to the man's earnings.

Other interviewees and their families were dependent on others: *I've got a grandma who lives here next to me and she helps me, as simple as that. I can always count on her and whenever I'm having tough time, she would always give me a hand* (M/2). *Actually my mother-in-law maintains us, so to speak. My mom, my grandma gave me money to buy diapers for a baby but it is really hard* (ZB/2).

A common household was maintained when mother's/ grandmother's flat was shared with daughter/granddaughter and her children. Expenses were then incurred depending on who has some cash at the moment: *I will help when I have money, they will help when they have money. We simply help each other. Whenever we do shopping we share everything, we're doing everything to-*

gether, lunches, breakfasts are shared (Z/2). It seemed that unmarried women with children were still treated by their mothers/grandmothers as children who happened to become mothers. No financial contribution was expected from them and their family allowance and welfare benefit were treated as an additional contribution to family budget. Presumably this was the case since the interviewees became mothers as teenagers and also because of the lack of wedding: there was no rite of passage from childhood to adulthood. Formation of a family of procreation as a result of motherhood did not separate them from their family of origin. They did not leave their original home turning it into an 'empty nest'. On the contrary, they filled it by moving in with their own child. It is noteworthy that the interviewees themselves accepted their status in the family of origin since *parents will always help you*. Mothers/grandmothers run the household. They decided about spending, shopping and money. Staying at parents'/grandparents' home protects against financial crises since elder women know how to manage money and they are thrifty. Young mothers who rented a flat together with their husbands or occupied social housing were in a more difficult situation. They could not afford running costs of housing since most often they were both unemployed and lived on social benefits: *I have to pay 300 zloty for electricity and how am I supposed to do that? It is simply hard, really hard* (ZB/2). *You don't even want to go out since when you go out with a child, the child will always ask for something and she is too little to explain it to her that there is no money for that. You have to have money to buy her even a lollipop* (E/2). Benefits were the key source of young women's and their children's livelihood although it was humiliating for them to apply for welfare benefits: *Frankly speaking, I've had enough of begging, of all of this. It makes you cry. You have to beg for everything, they are doing you a favour everywhere. When I go to this welfare and I have to beg for everything and they want you to make copies of the piles of papers, you bring them and then it turns out they don't need half of them* (M/2).

The biographies of the women of the younger generation in most cases have been marked by the traumatic experience from the childhood caused by alcoholism of their fathers, sometimes of both parents, which resulted in bad financial conditions as well as in violence, aggression, the lack of conditions to learn, and ultimately in serious problems at school and the need for turning for help to their grandparents'.

The biographical experience of the women of the younger generation is also marked by the fact that they started short-lasting relationships at a young age, which often resulted in unplanned and accidental pregnancies. Due to the low level of education and the early motherhood, they remained unemployed, and consequently had to depend on the social security system as their main source of income.

Chapter 5

Poverty in the biographical experience of women from the youngest generation – 'granddaughters'[1]

The biographies of women presented in this chapter have not been collected within the same research project as the biographies of women presented in the previous parts of the book. The 'granddaughters' are not really related to 'daughters', 'mothers' and 'grandmothers', whose life stories were reconstructed and analysed earlier. Nevertheless, the 'granddaugh-

1 The youngest generation – 'granddaughters' is represented by eleven women aged nineteen or twenty. At the time interviews took place, each of them had one child (four months to two years old). One of them was married. The other ten had complicated and unclear relationships with their partners/fathers of their babies. Even when they declared they were in an intimate relationship with a man, those men were usually away (for example, working in another city, in jail, staying with their relatives) and they were not living together at the time of the research. Therefore, it was difficult to make clear distinction whether they were in non-marital relationships or not. Officially, for the information of social service workers, all of the interviewees, except for the married one, were reported as single. In most cases, their children had the mothers' family names and in their birth certificates it was declared that their fathers were unknown. In some cases it was true – the fathers had gone before the babies were born and did not remain in touch with young mothers.

The 'granddaughters' had their children at the age of sixteen to nineteen. Of eleven women, three graduated from 6-year elementary school, six graduated from a three-year gymnasium (second stage in Polish educational system), one graduated from vocational school and one had had high school education, but did not take the final graduation exam (so called 'matura' or 'maturity exam' which allows to go to college). One of the interviewed women had a registered job at the time of the interview – she was working in a factory, being employed by a temporary work agency. One was on parental leave she was entitled to, as she had been in a job training program at the time she was pregnant. The other women had very limited work experience – some had unregistered temporary jobs before they got pregnant, or during pregnancy. Welfare and family benefits were the main source of maintenance for the 'granddaughters', along with modest financial support of either parents, grandparents, or partners.

ters' might just as well have been the daughters of the representatives of the 'daughters' generation born in the mid-70s. Their real mothers and grandmothers shared the same socio-economical profile as the women described earlier in the book.

The 'granddaughters' were born in the years 1989 and 1990. When the interviews took place, they were 18 or 19 years of age, all living in Łódź poverty pockets. Some of them had lived in different parts of the city in their childhood (in the so-called 'blocks of flats', offering much better housing conditions than the devastated tenement buildings in the city centre) and moved into poverty pockets as school-aged kids; others were brought up in the pocket of poverty from the very beginning of their lives. All the eleven individuals representing the youngest generation of women form poverty pockets in this book had already been mothers when the research was done. They became pregnant and gave birth to their first children as teenagers. Their life stories were collected within the 'WZLOT – Strengthening Opportunities and Weakening the Intergenerational Transmission of Poverty' project at the turn of the years 2008 and 2009. The project ran by the Department of Applied Sociology and Social Work of the University of Łódź was focused on mechanisms of poverty and social exclusion transmission viewed from intra- and intergenerational perspectives, on spatial concentration of poverty, and on social policy responses to these problems. The research part of the project involved the assessment of the particular situation at which specific groups at risk of poverty and social exclusion found themselves, both in the city of Łódź and in the Łódź region. As teenage parenthood is considered an important risk factor causing or enhancing material deprivation and social isolation, one of the WZLOT project's research modules explored early parenthood in deprived neighbourhoods of a post-industrial city, exemplified by Łódź. Within this module, the researches collected one hundred interviews on the life stories of young women and men who had become parents in their teens. Below, eleven of them were brought into analysis.

Women of the 'granddaughters' generation were born in the years 1989 and 1990. They have never experienced life in the era of real socialism. The life stories of the interviewees mirror the processes and phenomena characteristic of the last decade of the 20th and the first decade of the 21st century in the Polish society such as: weakening family bonding (divorces, fragile interfamily ties), decline of man and fatherhood (missing fathers, missing partners, women taking all responsibility for the children), alienation of youth (leading to taking up risk behaviours), precarisation of labour market (occasional work, temporary work, unregistered work, employment by temporary work agencies, politics of outsourcing, lack of entitlement to paid holidays, sick leave or termination notice period, disrespect of labour law and employees rights), privatization of children (withdrawal of public agencies from provision of generally available services allowing for reconciliation of family and professional life, such as free or inexpensive childcare), transformation from welfare into workfare and the illusiveness of social policy responses to the threat of social exclusion (i.e. training courses and programs for the unemployed not really improving their opportunities on the labour market), underfunding and partial privatization of health care system (division into paid higher quality health care services and state-guaranteed lower quality health care services), and the overall development of market-driven economy as such (wherein workforce of unskilled physical workers is of little value).

The women described in this chapter were all teenage mothers. Teenage motherhood in Western, developed societies is being associated by social researchers to problems of poverty and social exclusion (Berthoud, Robson 2001; UNICEF 2001). Poverty and social exclusion are seen as both: the cause and the consequence of teenage parenthood (Teenage Parenthood Independent Advisory Group, 2008; The Working Group on Teenage Pregnancy and Parenthood 2000; Wiggins et al. 2005, Berthoud, Robson 2001; UNICEF 2001). The highest teenage pregnancy rates characterize the most unequal societies (Wiggins et al. 2005). The factors associated with early pregnancy and early childbearing include: low socio-economic status of family of origin, inhabiting poor, socially deprived neighbourhood, living in social housing, growing up in a monoparental family, parent's divorce (especially if the break-up takes place when the girl is aged 5 or less), being the eldest daughter of teenage mother, having experienced sexual violence, having parents (and especially mother) not interested in daughter's educational career, low educational attainment, problems at school, so-called 'low expectations', having started smoking early, early sexual initiation, and many others (Ermisch 2003; Immamura et al. 2006; Arai 2009). Most of these factors are present in biographies of the interviewed young women.

What is very characteristic of life stories of the 'granddaughters' presented in this chapter is the lack of men figures. Grandfathers do not play any role in young women's memories, only grandmothers are being recalled. Fathers, if they are still alive, were the families' trouble makers and often have disappeared (left, started new family, went to prison). Most of the partners and fathers of the interviewees' babies do not take responsibility for their offspring. Even when they claim they love and care, for various reasons they stay away from their children and their mothers. Although the interviewed women were trying hard to speak well about their children's fathers, oftentimes they would confess their partners were violent, drinking, drug abusing, involved in suspicious activities. It was meaningful what one of the interviewed women said about the prospect future of her 7-month old son: *I just wish he'd never go to jail, not to jail* (M/63).

The 'granddaughters' generation share many life experiences with the 'daughters' generation, such as disorganisation of life in families of origin, early termination of education and unemployment, and early motherhood. In opposition to the previous generation, their early pregnancies were not unplanned. For the representatives of the youngest generation of women from the poverty pockets, getting pregnant was not 'an accident'. None of the respondents used contraception at time they got pregnant. Some of the interviewed women clearly expressed they had planned to get pregnant. Others said they were absolutely aware of the possibility of getting pregnant. It seems that in unstable world with limited opportunities motherhood may become a life strategy, a path interviewees chose for themselves, not really being conscious of what it may bring to them.

The formative biographical experiences of the generation of the 'granddaughters' which led to poverty and dependence are related to:

1) in childhood period: multiple problems in the family of origin (such as break-ups and divorces, interfamily violence, sudden job losses and unemployment, debts, deaths and sicknesses);
2) in adolescence period: learning problems, isolation in school environment, inability to meet teachers' demands, strong negative influence of peer group, taking up risk behaviours, early pregnancy;
3) in early adulthood: teenage (and mostly single) motherhood, dependency on family of origin and/or social welfare system, exclusion from education and labour market, extremely poor housing conditions.

1. Childhood

1.1. Good childhood memories

Among the representatives of the 'granddaughters' generation there are two groups to be distinguished. Women belonging to the first one have good childhood memories: they remember a modest but happy life in a family securing material and emotional stability. They usually lived with both parents (sometimes also grandparents or just grandmothers), oftentimes in rather small apartments equipped with all necessary facilities such as central heating, running hot water, toilet and bathroom, in one of the Łódź panel housing (many of these were built in the socialist era on the outskirts). Women recall their parents working a lot. Parents were so busy their daughters were mostly under grandmothers' supervision. *Parents were working all the time. Grandma and grandpa raised us* (M/35); *My dad was working, my mom was working, we lived with the grandma. We had two rooms and a kitchen in a block of flats* (M/32). Interviewed women belonging to this group remember light-heartedness, playing with their friends in the backyards, good neighbour-to-neighbour relations, the warmth their family (probably mostly their grandmothers) gave them. At certain point in their childhood a crisis would come. It could have been one misfortunate occurrence (such as parent's divorce, sickness, job loss, debts) or a combination of all of them. Parent's divorce was leading to a loss of contact with one of the parents, usually with the father (although two of the interviewed women were raised by fathers after their parents split up). Usually in the mid or late-90s, i.e. when the girls were in the pre-school or already school age, they would move into a tenement house in a poverty pocket, where the housing conditions and the type of neighbours were much different to what they had experienced before, but where it was cheaper to live. *Before, I lived in a better neighbourhood, in a better area* (M/35), as they used to describe in interviews. It is difficult to identify one predominant reason for removals. Respondents did not know why they had had to move, this was probably never clearly explained to them. They only realized they needed to adjust to new circumstances and living conditions. As one of the women commented, *it was my mom's decision, that's it* (M/38).

1.2. Childhood trauma

The second group of young women representing the 'granddaughters' generation suffered from traumatic experiences, usually resulting from alcohol abuse of either their fathers, or their both parents. As one of the interviewees said about her childhood: *I hope my son will never go through what I went through* (M/63). The respondents experienced severe material poverty, understood as scarcity of goods and financial means. As one of the women, whose father was an alcohol addict and whose brother was drug addict recalls: *I always envied my friends, they had so many toys, so much of everything, and I could not have had that. My mom counted every penny (...) and my brother would take away everything from our home* [to sell for drugs] (M/22). Also, their poverty had every other else-than material dimensions, also identified in biographies of earlier generations of women from poverty enclaves. For example, as very young girls, some of the interviewees were expected to take care of younger siblings and household. They were children growing up taking on adult responsibilities: *I was taking care of my sister, when I was a kid, all the time. My mom was working late every day, so I am very good at all the housekeeping stuff such as cleaning, taking care of children, all that, because I was taking care of my sister. In primary school, in the first grade, I was taking her to preschool, bringing her back home, cleaning, cooking, on regular basis* (M/22).

Poverty led to the necessity of changing place of residence quite often: *We were moving all the time, we had no permanent place to stay. Our mom, she was renting* [flats, rooms, etc.] (…) *Now she has debts, big amounts of money to pay back, loans, I don't really know* [how much] (M.22). [My childhood] *wasn't good at all. I was in a foster care. My mom is an alcoholic, my dad is in jail. We were raised by our grandma. A little bit in here, a little while in there… different places. The streets raised me, so to say. Those worse streets* (M/50).

One research participant summarized her childhood in three words: *Poverty and violence* (M/63). She did not want to add anything else, she avoided talking about her childhood and especially about her father. Three women from the 'granddaughters' generation were put into foster care as children because their parents' parental rights were limited or taken away. One of them went into an institutional foster care and the others were put into related foster families which were their grandmothers. Being formally put into grandmother's family has not resulted in any improvement as regards their difficult social environment. It is also worth stressing that most of these women moved in with their parents (or siblings) again after they gave birth to a child. It means that to raise their own child they went back to the environment where they had experienced their own childhood trauma.

The only woman that was sent to a children's institution recalls: *My childhood was very complicated. Jesus, where to start from… I'll start with this: I didn't stay too long at home. My parents were fighting (…) I was the youngest one, my sister got married and moved out and I stayed alone* [with parents]. *The parents were fighting. I went to school. Actually I wasn't going to school for some time because there was no one to walk me to school and bring me back from school. I was seven, eight years old. I was in primary school. I had to sleep at our neighbour's. My parents were telling me to leave. They were drinking and they didn't like when I was crying. Because when they were fighting I was horrified and I was crying, and they would throw me out. I'd sleep on a staircase. That neighbour of ours, she would take me in, she became interested* [in the situation at home]. *She called the police: once, twice, three times. Finally, the family court became interested, too. My mom was called into court. She did not show up. I was raised in a residential care institution* (M/58).

The interviewees' families were multi-child ones (up to five siblings). The women would often recall mothers and grandmothers who also had many brothers and sisters (up to eight). In families where the family bond was not broken, siblings became a valuable source of support in the situation of early motherhood. However, among the interviewees there were women who did not know where their sisters and brothers were (the same applies to fathers who divorced their mothers). There were also women who did not want to know what is going on with their closest relatives (for example with an alcoholic mother who after two strokes was put into a shelter for the homeless).

2. Adolescence

2.1. Early disengagement from school – hanging out with *those guys*

In the period of early adolescence biographies of all women representing the 'granddaughter' generation become similar, characterized mainly by dislike of school and isolation in educational environment. All of the interviewed women around 5th or 6th grade of primary school (so at the age of 12 or 13) began having serious learning problems and started to play truant. Some avoided school because they performed very poorly and felt they were unable to catch-up with school material. Because of what was happening at home, they had no chance to prepare for school, to do their homework: *School? I was never interested in school. I was never told to do anything related with school [at home]. I wasn't looked after. Maybe if I had know I needed to learn it would have been different?* [at home] *it was always loud, crowdy, there was drinking, no conditions for learning* (M/50). Some even liked school at the beginning but at certain moment education was no longer attractive to them: *Well, I just did not feel like going* [to school] *anymore* (M/38).

In every life story early adolescence is landmarked when the interviewed girls meet *these guys*. New friends of the same age and sometimes a few years older become their reference group and hugely influence their lives. The peer group becomes a diversion from their families and school problems. Interviewees report spending a lot of time with their friends: *In gymnasium* [secondary school] *I played truant a lot. I didn't move up* [to the next class]. *I started missing school, hanging out with these guys... I'd got a guardian. I lost all my interest in learning. I really enjoyed not going to school so much! My friends wouldn't go so I wouldn't go either.* (M/35). *I've always had older friends. These girls were already of age, they would go to parties, clubs, they had boyfriends and... I hung out with this kind of people and I wanted to be like them. I would tell my mom I was going to sleep at my friend's but really I was going somewhere else to a party. And I got what I wanted. In the end, I wasn't a bad girl. I wasn't drinking, I wasn't smoking, I wasn't fighting or something like this. I was just hanging out with older guys who could do everything because they were adults and I couldn't because I was a minor. And what happened, happened...* [the pregnancy] (M/22). *My mom wanted me to graduate but I didn't (...) I met those guys (...) Now I really regret it because if I stayed in school, maybe I'd have a job now (...) It wasn't a good company for me (...) it was a company with drinking and drug using. I wasn't using, I was drinking, drinking really absorbed me, going to clubs, coming back late, that's why I wasn't going to school* (M/63).

Those who left school for good before getting pregnant did not seek for permanent job. They were trying different ways of earning money: waitering, bartending, being a shop assistant, never officially registered by their employers. One of interviewees recalls life before pregnancy like this: *Well, a little bit of work. And a lot of partying* (M/38).

2.2. Early pregnancy

Studies on family formation patterns in poverty pockets point to early motherhood as source of positive identity, respect and opportunity to take up a positive, highly praised social role for young women of low socio-economic status. Critical studies on teenage parenthood present teenage mothers from disadvantaged social spaces as those who by having children early decide to take 'fast line to adulthood' because they cannot expect success in slow transition to adulthood (characteristic for middle class, involving long education, development of professional career, marriage, and then having a child) (Graham, McDermott 2006). As Mary Erdmans and Tim Black put it, *motherhood is a mark of achievement – not just for teen mothers but also for most women; it fulfills expectations and provides a source of status* (Erdmans, Black 2015: 29). The above-quoted authors also refer to studies by Linda Burton, who claims early motherhood might be a successful life-course strategy in poor communities where health problems are common and where there are very few 'marriageable' men and little job opportunities. Having a child early (when still healthy) within extended multigenerational family is a reasonable choice young women make (Burton after: Erdmans, Black 2015: 33). For women with traumatic childhood experiences, motherhood can be a 'self-affirming' strategy and an opportunity to 'start over' (Erdmans, Black 2015: 138), cut off the distressed past and begin with something new and pure. Psychologist Jane Music puts it briefly: *If adolescent did not want babies, they would not have them* (Music 1993: 109).

The fathers of the babies were either the peers of the interviewees or they were significantly older. Boys of the same age were usually met for the first time in the neighborhood, in a club, at a party, not long before getting pregnant. With the older men (usually five, eight or even fourteen years older) the interviewed women usually had had a couple-of-years long relationship before they got pregnant. It means that their intimate relations began when the girls were thirteen or fourteen years old.

In case of early motherhood, it is very difficult to make clear statements determining pregnancy intentions (Ellis-Sloan 2012: 140). Teenage pregnancies are not easily divided into 'planned' and 'unplanned' categories as there is a lot of ambivalence involved (ibid.). Among the interviewees, some of the women decidedly specified their pregnancies as planned. Other pregnancies, if not planned, definitely were not avoided. None of the interviewees used contraception at the time they got pregnant. In fact, those who had been using contraception before (for example who were on pill) stopped using contraception when they started being intimate with their partners who became babies' fathers: *I just stopped taking pills. I don't know why I stopped, I just did (...) I think I was meant to get pregnant and I just did* (M/32).

A 17-year old mother described in an interview how she planned to have a child. She told her partner (she was 16 years old at the time he moved in with her and her mother) she was on pill while she was not. She got pregnant and told him about it immediately. He was surprised but quickly accepted the news and they decided to get married. Marriage had to be allowed for by family court as she was not of age at that time. When she was 4 months pregnant, they moved out from her mother's and started living independently, renting a very small flat (with no bathroom and toilet in the corridor, shared with other neighbours). The court granted a marriage permission and they became husband and wife just a few days before their son was born. At the time the interview was done, they were living together and she seemed to be very happy. The husband was a son of the interviewees mother's friend. Hard working, with a steady, relatively well-paid job, without any criminal record seemed to be a good 'catch' in comparison to other young males form poverty pocket. The women's decision might have been a strategy to make him stay with her. However, asked by an interviewer whether she had considered single motherhood (she could not be sure how he would react to the perspective of becoming a father), she said *she cared about a baby more than about a husband* (M/06) and that first of all, she wanted to have a baby. Asked why had she wanted a baby so much she answered she *wanted to have something to do* (M/06).

Another women reported: *I was with this guy. We'd been together for five years already. So I decided to have a baby, and so it happened. We were living together already, I moved into his place, and so I got* [pregnant]... *We wanted that. I did, he did. It wasn't an accident* (M/63). Other women were less explicit about planning on having a baby. However, they also admitted they were thinking of getting pregnant. *I had 'preparation for family life' class at school*[2]*. And they told us there are no methods 100% safe. My friend's sister was on pill and she got pregnant. Another friend was sick, had an obstructed ovaries, and she got pregnant (...). So, when you are to get pregnant, you get pregnant. When your hormones are strong, there's no way to stop it* [getting pregnant] (M/32).

Usually, young women in the study did not really suspect they were pregnant until they missed one or two periods (so when they were about 3 months pregnant). In some cases, however, pregnancy was confirmed extremely late: *I did not notice anything until the 6th-7th month. My mom noticed* [her being pregnant]. *She bought me a pregnancy test. I couldn't believe it (...). I had no pregnancy symptoms. I felt much better[pregnant] than before. I lost a lot of weight at the beginning* [of the pregnancy] (M/35). *I only went to a doctor for the first time when I was in my 23rd week* (M/20). This can be interpreted as denial of pregnancy. Some authors, however, point to the fact that adolescents' menstrual cycle might be too irregular to discover pregnancy and that the word 'denial' should be rather replaced by 'unsuspecting' (Erdmans, Black 2015: 195). Other authors see young pregnant women's behaviour as expression of fear, embarrassment and being afraid to confront the reality of pregnancy (Hudson, Ineichen 1991 after: Ellis-Sloan 2012: 161).

2 A form of sexual education, family and natural contraception methods oriented.

3. Early adulthood

3.1. Single teenage motherhood

Most of the women representing the 'granddaughters' generation recalled the delivery of their first baby as something extremely painful and scary, almost to the point of being unbearable. A few of them asserted that they would never have a child again, just because they do not want to go through labour again. Maybe it was so because they were often alone in a hospital, not assisted by their partner nor by their mother, or a friend. The moment of giving birth to a baby was also deprived of intimacy – usually they were observed and sometimes assisted by groups of medicine students or young doctors in training. Some of them were also looked down on and openly criticized for starting a family too early. One of the interviewees recalled a doctor (maybe a professor, maybe the head of the ward as this happened during the usual morning round) telling her in front of numerous residents and students: *You are too young to be a mother!* She remembered being powerful enough to respond: *And you're too old to be a doctor!* (M/06).

A few women reported delaying the moment of going to hospital as long as they could. *I gave birth 2 days after I was supposed to. I had already had labour cramps, I just didn't know it was labour cramps, because it was very painful in here* [shows where]. *I just thought I was in pain. So I went to a doctor. And it turned out I had been in labour, for two days* (M/35). It may point to the fact that the young women were not prepared for the moment of labour: neither in terms of knowledge (they did not know the symptoms of forthcoming delivery), nor emotionally – it seems they were afraid of labour and of what was going to happen afterwards, so they ignored the sings. Another respondent said she had not prepared anything for the baby before it was born: she had no newborn clothes, her room was painted by her father 2 days before her leaving the hospital. Maybe she had not been sure whether she was going to keep the baby. None of the interviewed women took part in parenting classes (that prepare parents-to-be not only for newborn care, but also for delivery)[3]. None of them mentioned considering adoption[4].

3 At the time research was carried there were no free parenting classes in Łódź available.

4 As teenage motherhood researcher Kyla Ellis-Sloan point out (2012: 164), adoption in our matherhood discourse is for 'bad' mothers; it is only something a 'bad' women would do.

Having delivered a baby (or in some cases in the earlier times, during pregnancy) those of the interviewed women who had previously moved out and started living with their boyfriends or were in foster care – moved back with their family of origin. The help provided by mothers (or, in a few cases - by fathers, grandmothers, older sisters) turned out to be of high value. The interviewees admitted they handed over child care and household work in large extent to their mothers (or fathers). They also disclosed that it is much easier and more comfortable for them to stay with their parents than at their boyfriend's. *You know, when you live by yourself, you have to do everything by yourself. Cooking, cleaning, washing... So you know, when I was there* [at boyfriend's place], *it was tiring. No one helped me doing every day work so it wasn't that bad to come back. My mom takes him* [the son] *when I want to sleep longer, because he wakes up at 5 a.m. (...). I don't have to cook at all because she is doing all the cooking, also for him* [for the baby]. *When she's here, I don't have to do anything in the kitchen* (M/04).

The 'granddaughter's' mothers (and in some cases fathers, grandmothers or older sisters) were often the ones who would get up early in the morning when the babies woke up, they accompanied young mothers during sleepless nights when babies were crying, they would do the shopping, cooking, and other housework. *Generally, my mom showed me everything and told me what to do* [with the baby]. *She's not living with us* [after divorce the interviewee stayed with her father and her mother moved out] *but she came to live in here for a month after the baby was born (...). Because at the beginning I didn't even know how to prepare baby formula* (M/35). *My mom did more around the baby then I did. I was just sitting there* [during the childbed period] (M/63). Parents or grandmothers would also stay with the baby when young mothers wanted to go out. [Living with grandmother] *is ok. We have our own room. Whenever we want to go out, grandma takes care of the baby* (M/29). Most of the interviewees asserted that having a child did not make their circle of friends shrink. Some even said that because of the baby they had a chance to meet new people who also had babies. The interviewees stressed that having a child at their age is nothing extraordinary in their social environment: most of their peer female friends, or even younger girls, are either pregnant, or already bearing a child. *This year practically half of my friends had their babies* (M/35). *All my friends already got pregnant, either at the same time I did or even earlier. One of them is twenty one and she's already got two children* (M/63).

Living with the family of origin was also less costly: *I don't buy food, because my dad is always buying. Now he's got a girlfriend and she's always asking me what to buy and she goes* [to a store] *and buys what I say*

(M/20). Women who were still under age were under legal guardianship of their parents, which also meant the parents could have applied for family benefits for them.

A recurrent theme in women's narrations on their babies and mothering was giving up breastfeeding (or not taking it up at all). The sole one of eleven interviewees who was breastfeeding did this for the first three months after the baby was born. She said the baby was sick all the breastfeeding time and when she decided to switch into baby formula, suddenly the child became healthy (M/32). *Oh no, he* [the son] *had no colic. When I got back home* [from the hospital] *I weaned him from the breast. I started feeding him with the bottle (...) I did not want* [to breastfeed]. *My mom said it's too exhausting... I preferred to wean him. I had him drink the formula from the very beginning, especially that it was for free*[5]. *And he was growing up normally. He's not sick or anything* (M/63). All interviewees said that since being 6 months old, their children eat basically the same things adults eat (mostly soups). There are no separate dishes for children and adults prepared. Children's diet was supplemented with babies desserts such as yogurts.

Another frequently mentioned issue was babies and children being very quiet, almost invisible: not waking up at nights (not even for feeding), not crying, playing by themselves. *It is so great because she* [the daughter, 8 months old] *was sleeping all nights since she was born. She is so quiet. No one even noticed that something had changed* [after the baby was born]. *She doesn't cry at all, she doesn't whine, even when she's having her teeth grow. She's here, but it's like she wasn't here at all, she's so quiet* (M/35). *She* [the daughter, 5 months old] *doesn't wake up at night. For example, she goes to bed at 7 in the evening, and she sleeps until 7 in the morning. All night long. And if she goes to sleep at ten, she gets up at half past eight... and sometimes even eleven. It depends* (M/20). *He* [the son, 7 months old,] *sleeps like a log at night. He also sleeps during the day* (M/63).

Most of the interviewed women admitted that because of their early motherhood they did not have a chance to let off steam. *I've lost my youth. Because when you already have a baby, it is the baby all the time* (M/22). *I didn't even have time to let off steam. I've just turned eighteen. Before, my father didn't let me go out. I was thinking: once I turn eighteen, I'll go crazy, I'll be partying, going everywhere (...) Unfortunately, that didn't happen* (M/35). Young mothers missed their previous social life, parties, seeing friends regularly. Nevertheless, talking about their present lives they often mentioned going out in the evenings, having children care secured by mothers, fathers, grandmothers, cousins etc. At least in some cases having a baby wasn't a barrier to continuation of social life.

5 Social welfare clients can obtain baby formula for free in special pharmacies.

As most mothers of every age do, the interviewed women experience ambivalence in their motherhood. They expressed not just satisfaction, but also the feeling of being overburdened with their new role: *Well, the best part is that I can see her laughing, being happy, I can play with her. The worst and most difficult part is that I have to sit with her all the time and pay attention, and care for her. I cannot go to a party as I used to go, I cannot get back home late. I had to quit school, I have to think of getting a job so that she has something to eat, so that she has everything she needs. I cannot think about myself only, I need to think of a child* (M/35).

The most difficult cases were those of two women who had been in foster care and could not count on any support from their parents, grandparents and boyfriends: *They were right, those who said I would regret it* [having a baby] (M/50). *I am afraid of what is going to happen. That I won't make it (...) That I won't have enough money, that I won't pay for something, that I'll forget about something important (...). No, that baby came too soon. Definitely too soon* (M/58).

3.2. On the margins of the labour market

Only one out of eleven respondents had a job at the time research was done. She was employed by temporary work agency in a large production plant. She was living with her (not the baby's) father, who was taking care of her daughter when she was at work. Nevertheless, the young mother was planning to find a nursery because the grandfather could not resist and kept giving sweets to the 8-month old girl so she was very overweight, which was stated by their paediatrician. Another young mother was on parental leave and was entitled to small benefit because she had been taking part in vocational training when she got pregnant.

The other women were social welfare clients, registered at the Employment Office. Some made attempts to take up work but it was not easy to combine it with early motherhood: *There was a time I got a job. It was 2,5 hrs a day. But soon I realised it is too much because... It was cleaning. I had to go a long way. So first, I had to bring* [my son] *to my mom's to leave him with her, afterwards I had to go to pick him up. So it wasn't paying off, not for this money, not with all this travelling. So at that time M.* [the name of the baby's father] *was, let's say, working, and I was at home, alone. Now I cannot move out* [from my parents] *because I cannot go to work. So as long as he's gone* [in jail] *I'm on social welfare* (M/04).

All interviewees were planning to get a job and most of them wanted to go back to school. They had very little work experience: *At the vocational school I did a job training at* [the name of a popular chain of delis],

I worked for a while in a grocery store, later, when I was pregnant, I was earning some money in a car wash, cleaning cars, and now I stay at home, I am on welfare. Young mothers' employment plans were always dependant on finding a nursery for their children[6]. Also, they always planned to start realizing their plans in a couple of months or years time. *I want to go to work, when she's 12 months. I want to put her to a nursery, then.* (M/20). *I'll go to sigh her up for the nursery in February, so that in September I could go back to school and in the end of next year find a job* (M/32).

Some of the women were very clear they did not wanted to *leave the baby* (M/06) and they would start looking for a job only when the child is already in pre-school, meaning at least three years old. At least a few of the interviewees participated labour market activisation projects provided by Social Welfare Centre or by Employment Office. *Only recently I was in training offered by the welfare office, it was learning to prepare invoices. I finished it, I have a certificate. Maybe I can find a job with it?* (M/22).

3.3. Undignifying housing conditions

The interviewed women and their children lived in extremely poor housing conditions. They either used commune housing (apartments under the city of Łódź administration and being rented to citizens) or social housing (very inexpensive and usually substandard apartments for the poorest). Their housing conditions were characterised by: little and overcrowded space (seven people in two small rooms, for instance), lack of bathroom and toilet, lack of running hot water, heating system expensive in maintenance. The apartments were cold but also humid, walls often attacked by fungus.

Even if respondents were trying to upgrade their living space conditions, the buildings (old devastated tenement houses) of their apartments were in such bad condition that home improvements made little sense. For example, one of the interviewees renovated floor and walls and painted the whole flat (it was a room with small kitchen and a corridor, social housing). Soon improvements were destroyed because the roof was leaking and the ceiling fell down.

Below there are exemplary descriptions of the housing conditions of the young women and their families. Notes were provided by the re-

6 At the time the research was carried, about 3% of Polish children aged less that 3 years were in institutional day care (nurseries) (UNICEF 2013: 13). In the years 2008/2009 63,1% of children aged 3 to 6 were in pre-school education in Poland (ibid.: 14).

searchers, since the interviews were carried at the homes of the respondents: *The apartment consists of two big rooms. One of the room was divided into two parts with a furniture. First part is a kitchen, the second one – the room occupied by the parents of the respondent room. It is very modest, equipped with time-worn bed, armchair and coffee table, a TV-set. Kitchen furniture is also ruined. The second room belongs to the interviewee, her baby and her two younger sisters. It is much more pleasant. There is no bathroom and no toilet in the apartment* (M/63).

The apartment the interviewee lives in at the moment belongs to her sister. There are seven people in total living there: interviewee's sister with her husband and two children, the interviewee's brother and the interviewee herself with her baby. The apartment consists of three rooms: connecting kitchen and two bedrooms. The smaller bedroom belongs to the interviewee's sister and her husband. They have a big bed, a closet, a desk, a TV-set and a computer in there. In the second, much larger room there is a coffee table and two [convertible] armchairs. It is the bedroom of the interviewee, her baby, her brother and two nieces. The interviewee sleeps in one bed with her brother and her baby. The apartment was clean, cosy and very nicely decorated. Unfortunately, it has no bathroom or toilet (M/58).

A social apartment, granted to interviewee's grandmother who left for Scotland with her partner (to work there). Situated at the ground floor. You enter it through huge heavy wooden doors with no handle or a doorbell. Then, there is a small corridor, completely blind, with no light bulb. Behind it there is the apartment which is one small room. The room which also plays the role of a kitchen, is very modest. There is a sink and a kitchen cabinet, an old destroyed stove that is out of order, an old fridge, an old TV-set (and DVD player), a radio, a convertible sofa (used as a bed). The only good looking pieces of furniture are a new closet and a cupboard. The interviewee has one old shabby pot. The room is extremely cold. One of the windows is broken. Behind the window there is a little square where people pass all the time. In the evening people gather there to drink alcohol. It is loud in there. There is no bathroom and toilet. The interviewee claimed she and her partner had no access to the bathroom and toilet. She says she and her partner relieve themselves into plastic bags and throw them out into the garbage (M/50).

The apartment is dark, shabby and clattered up with things. It consists of a corridor, a kitchen, toilet and two bedrooms. The rooms are so small and cramped with things that practically there is no place to sit there. The room is narrow and long. There is a huge wall unit on one side and there is a coffee table, bed and armchair on the other side, a TV-set and a DVD player. The room is full of everything, for example there is a huge potato bag in the middle of it. Similarly in the kitchen: no place to move, there is a fridge, kitchen furniture, something like an armchair, a little sofa, the baby's carriage. There is no baby bed in the apartment. It is hard to imagine more than two people living in space small like this, especially with a small baby (M/20).

Those of the young women who moved into poverty pocket at a certain moment of their lives, and remember living in better conditions, were very critical about their housing conditions: *We are living here like in some kind of slum* (M/38). All of the interviewed women were hoping for some improvement of their housing conditions. As they could not afford buying or renting a flat on the free housing market, they were expecting to obtain a commune or social apartment just for themselves and their babies so that they would not have to share limited living space with so many people. However, an average waiting time for a social apartment in Łódź, at the time interviews were done, was about 6-7 years. Those put the foster care were in a privileged situation, as provision of social housing for them was treated as priority and they were usually given social apartments soon after leaving foster care institution.

3.4. Future plans

The way the young women spoke about their future proved their young age and showed little orientation in today's reality, especially as far as labour, education and housing market conditions are concerned. In some cases, asked about their future plans, the interviewees were taking about their dreams and fantasies rather than plans. For example, one of the respondents finished high school, but did not take final (so-called 'maturity') exams. Very reasonably, she wanted to take up office work, since it does not involve working shifts and its hours can be easily adjusted to the time when nurseries and preschools are open. However, her plan was to find a job in public administration such as the City Hall Office or Tax Office. Not only was she planning to work there only after passing her 'Matura' exams, but she also wanted to go to college to study administration and management and on obtaining her college certificate, she wanted a managerial position. *I want to pass my Matura exam, finish this stupid job training, go to college, find a job and put K.* [the daughter's name] *into a nursery. I'll go to office work when I'm done with my job training, and when I finish college I want a higher position, not just regular worker, I want to be the office manager* (M/32). Another woman [gymnasium graduate] also dreamt of high level posts: *Best job position for me is the manager* [laughter]. *And the perfect one would be if was a manger but working at home so that I could just sit at home while at work* (M/38).

Another young women was thinking of a career not for herself but for her newborn baby daughter: *When she's a bit older, I want to take her to one of those photo sessions... you can have your child in a commercial... I definitely want her have such a photo shooting. I'll also take her to dancing class, singing class so that she could get those skills and use them later on... I was going to such classes myself but then I gave it up, it was stupid of me...* (M/20). Another young woman's future plan was to buy an apartment in a block of flats where her son would live when he's adult. She wanted to have a second baby so she also wanted an apartment for him or her. Also, she said her family needs a summer house with a garden and a pond. She wanted her *children to have everything* because *it is not difficult to have children but it is an achievement to support them financially* (M/06).

There were also women whose reflections about their futures were more down-to-earth: *When you're a gymnasium graduate only, you cannot find a job. I would like to finish a school but I don't know what kind of school. Maybe it would be possible to go on weekends, or maybe in the evenings. But I have to wait until she's three. She'll go to pre-school. Maybe next year it will happen, maybe next year it all will better, finally (...) I would like to have a kind of job that I won't have to change it again and again* (M/22).

Many of the interviewed women mentioned planning on graduating from school (a gymnasium for adults or a high school). They wanted to go to general high school offering general education, with no specialization or vocational training. Also, they were thinking of going to private weekend or evening schools, offering very low quality education. Some were aware of the fact of graduating from these schools was of no use in the labour market: *I'll go to C.* [name of the school]. *Yeah, I think I'll go there. I've heard that later on employers look at diplomas from this school with a pinch of a salt, because you can just pay for everything and you don't have to study at all* (M/38).

For many respondents, the future was unclear. They had no plans, they were afraid of planning because everything they had already planned did not happened the way they wanted it to happen. Also, they felt left alone with the planning: *I live for today* [not making any plans]. *I'll be waiting until he* [the boyfriend] *gets out* [from jail]. *My only plan is to be with him. So that we can make plans together, not just me, myself* (M/04).

Young women were predominantly focused on their children and one's own role as a mother. Some already being pregnant decided to withdraw from activities such as school, work, anything other than family life: *God, how happy I was being pregnant. For me work wasn't important* (M/63). *I quit school only when I realized I was pregnant. Something could have happened to the belly* [someone may have pushed her or punch her by accident and hurt the feotus] *(...) I wanted to focus on pregnancy only* (...) *I want to keep him by myself all the time* (M/06). *Family is more important than friends (...). I'd rather be at home with my baby son and my husband than go anywhere* (M/06). *How could I leave him with someone and, for example, go to work? No, I am afraid that someone who stays with him would not care for him enough, that this person wouldn't do what should be done, for example put the cream for a nappy rash, go for a walk (...) give him medicines. A little baby like him has to go for a walk, doesn't he?* (M/50).

3.5. Women only

The 'granddaughters' were very much dependant on other women's support. *My mom helped me a lot and this is why* [the sickness of the baby daughter] *passed. I was alone but everyone supported me. My mom, grandma, my sister, my girlfriends* (M/22). Young mothers were surrounded and helped by another women. Men (with the exception of two fathers and two partners) were either gone, or not really taking up responsibilities.

Fathers of young women were usually gone since the interviewees were school-aged children. *So, my father* [a citizen of a country in South America] *was applying for a permanent residence card but he was refused and he went to Germany. Never got back. I haven't seen him for ten... eleven years. The last time I saw him was in Berlin, he took us for holidays for a month* [the interviewee and her sister witnessed their father being arrested by the German police; he was deported afterwards] (M/32). *I don't really care what is going on with him* [the father]. *I'm being honest with you. I haven't seen her for... I don't know, I was seven or eight...It's not important for me how he's doing. Let's leave him alone, living his own way* (M/38).

Fathers of the young women's babies were also usually gone. Even if they did not break up, they neither caring nor helpful. For example, a partner to one of the respondents and her baby's father used to punch her when she was pregnant. He drinks alcohol, smokes marihuana on every day basis, does not care about the baby, threatens the young woman. She wants him to leave but he is very comfortable in her grandmother's social apartment and does not want to go. In another case, a much older partner is married to another woman. He did not divorce her. He did not acknowledge the baby, the baby does not have the father's name. They used to live together, after the baby was born they had a fight and *he went back to his mama* (M/32).

A few of the interviewees babies fathers are in jail: *My ex-boyfriend is in jail (...) Had a car accident. He stole a car, with his boss and the bosses girlfriend, they were drinking. That girl was pregnant. And she lost the baby, had something wrong with an eye. [...]When he was arrested I was four or five months pregnant. He'll go for 5 to 8 years* [to prison] (M/63). The woman who had been in a children's home went to a boarding vocational school where she met the father of her baby. When she was pregnant and was about to leave school and children's home, she was removed to a facility for lone mothers (ran by nuns). She described what happened next: *So he went for winter holidays organized by the school. He met a girl there. I texted aunt Kasia* [in Polish children's homes children call their female tutors 'aunts'] *and she confirmed he hooked up an ugly girl. He told me she's just a friend. But everyone else told me they were dating. I was like how it is possible, he wouldn't do this, he's having a child. And it turned out to be true (...) I was asking him 'come back to me, leave her, take the baby'. But it was for nothing. (...) later on he asked me if he can visit us* [in the house ran by the sisters; the interviewee was waiting for social apartment she was granted as an ex-ward of institutional foster care]. *He'd come regularly. Everything was going well. But then he started drinking and stealing. He'd come drunk. He wouldn't give any money for the baby. He would bring stolen cell phones instead, saying 'go and sell it, you'll have diapers money'. There's nothing to hide. Later, he had the accident* (M/58).

Some women did not even want to see the babies' fathers: *I don't want him* [the baby's father] *have any rights and any contact* [with the daughter] *and nothing to do either with her or with me. I won't apply for alimonies because if I do, he will say he's got the right to see her. And he wouldn't pay, anyway* (M/35). Some fathers were gone to escape taking responsibility for the baby: *I haven't seen him ever since. I don't even know if he knows* [about the baby]. *He went somewhere, I don't know where. We are not in touch, I don't want any contact with him. (…) I was told he found out* [about me being pregnant]. *When I wanted to tell him, he disappeared. I couldn't find him. And then I just let it go. But I was told he found out and this was the reason why he disappeared, my friends told me (…) He's the kind of person that I don't want to have nothing in common with. I changed my mind about him* (M/22).

It is very clear that poverty and social exclusion experienced by the 'daughters' are being continued in the life stories of the 'granddaughters'. Biographies of representatives of both generations are shaped by similar problems: alcoholism, violence and neglect in the family of origin, school problems, exclusion from education and labour market, early family formation. Men cause troubles and disappear. Women are left alone and can only count on each other and social services.

The lives of women of the youngest generation, however, are strongly influenced by the outcomes of socio-economic transformation of the 1990s. Stories told by representatives of the 'granddaughters' generation also show the clash between the new active social policy model with its workfare approach and concentration on maternity as the one and only source of positive identity for the next generation of young women from poverty enclaves.

Chapter 6
Life histories of three families

The research that provided the basis for this book offers an opportunity that is seldom available in the Polish literature on the subject. It has allowed investigation of the life histories of members of the same family throughout a long period of time, from the childhood of today's grandmothers to the youth of their grandchildren, and even the childhood of their great-grandchildren. It has also allowed for identification of events in their descendants' lives that impacted or determined the history of their ascendants. This dynamic approach exposes the personal events that pushed them into poverty, leaving the social-historical context in the second plan.

Three families have been selected, and their life histories seem to represent three typical life paths, leading from poverty to poverty.

1. The F. family

'Feels like crying in this life. But life goes on. A dog in a kennel also keeps on living'

The F. family members represent a category of unqualified workers that was once a highly populace category in Łódź. Based on the relationships between the women of three consecutive generations, we were able to reconstruct this family's life history dating back to the inter-war period. Leokadia (born in 1918), who became a permanent resident of Łódź in 1947, is the founder of this family. She came to the city with her husband and two children. Previously they had lived in a village. She became a widow and a pensioner in 1978. She is the only member of the F. family who receives a regular and guaranteed income. Krystyna, her fifty-two year-old daughter, lives on social assistance benefits, just like Katarzyna, Leokadia's granddaughter, who is a single mother. Krystyna lives in a pocket of poverty, while Leokadia, with the granddaughter and her children, live in an apartment block built in the 1960s. The three generations have all experienced poverty, although at different times of their lives. Leokadia suffered poverty in childhood while her daughter and granddaughter in adulthood. Leokadia's living conditions in her adult years improved compared to her childhood, while her daughter's situation worsened, and she is currently on a trajectory of poverty. Leokadia was born in 1918 in a peasant family, which ran a farm on 15 *morgens* of sandy soil, in a small village composed of just sixteen families, where half of inhabitants were of German origin. Leokadia's mother was her father's second wife, and when the respondent was born, the father had already had three sons. Her mother died in 1919, leaving five sons and two daughters. After the mother's death, the father remarried for the third time, and had another six children. Therefore Leokadia had fifteen siblings, where six where younger than her. The father worked in the field and traded in horses. The soil was not fertile, however they had cows, a horse and poultry. They also bred pigs for which the children had to collect grass. The mother used to grow tomatoes and beetroot. On weekdays: *in the morning mother always cooked 'zacierki'* [wholemeal rye dumplings with milk], *borsht or 'zalewajka'* [a kind of potato soup cooked with sourdough], *we would not get a sandwich, bread or cold meat, as other families would get for their morning meal. We got the same food at lunchtime. She cooked whatever she had, bean or tomato soup, typical food at a farm.* Sunday lunches were better. The step-mother cooked chicken soup or bought a piece of meat from a farmer who had just slaughtered a pig. They had meat on weekdays, only when *something was just about to be wasted, if an animal died. Otherwise we were having* [meat], *only on Sundays, when mother bought it for Sunday lunch.* The family lived in harmony. Step-mother treated all the children equally. Father was an unquestionable authority to the children. Leokadia reports that her parents *taught us not to be naughty, not to fight and not to steal in particular, not to offend people, not to enter other people's property, not to steal from people's gardens or fields, not to damage their belongings and not to waste things. Our parents were strict with us, and no one ever complained to our father that this child did this, and that one did that, as if there were no children in this family. That is how we were brought up, father did not beat us, he only said one word and we understood. The work at the farm was also harmonious, if he told us to plough the field, the boys went to do this, if he told us to harrow, they were sowing, while the other boy was harrowing, we worked in such a harmony.* [Father] *never swore, never beat the mother, he would never call her names; I was not familiar with such behaviour.* The children were brought up in accordance with religious rules. All of the family members went to church. At home *everyone had to kneel and pray every morning and evening, we had to pray. Initially* [we were praying] *together, but once we learnt how to pray, everyone had to pray loudly for the parents to hear these prayers and check if we were saying the rights words. So our parents made sure that everyone had to go to church...during Lent, mum used to sing songs, and we were singing the religious songs, such as Bitter Sorrows and others, with her.*

Leokadia completed a seven-year elementary school, combining schoolwork with work on the farm. She was studying while grazing cows. Her younger brother covered for her when she was going to school. She left the family home when she was fourteen. She was 'given away to work as a servant' to a wealthier family, just like her elder brothers. Working as a servant meant that she had to live at her master's home. She could visit her family home on Sundays, after the church service (provided that she lived nearby), however she had to be back at the employer's home in the evening. On holidays, *all servants were going to their parents' and everyone was happy that it was holiday time, I went home for the holiday, and father received us so nicely.* She recollects: *I was working as a servant for two years. I stayed at one farmer's for a year, but I was not happy in this first place, as the farmer was dreadful, he kept beating his wife.* The farmer's wife and Leokadia had to run away from that house and spent the night in a haystack in the field. *Then another farmer employed me as he liked me because I was a good worker.* The respondent received room and board, and money for her work. Just like her brothers, she gave the money back to the parents who *had to take me to the city and buy necessary things for me, as I did not like to use clothes after my sister.* When she was sixteen, she left the employer unexpectedly, without letting her parents know, and went to Łódź. She left the village for fear of marriage – a relatively wealthy farmer had proposed to her, and threatened that if she did not marry him, he would kill her and then himself. Leokadia treated those threats seriously. She got on a bus and arrived in Łódź in 1934. She did not know anyone in the city. This is how she describes her arrival in Łódź: *I came to Łódź, maybe I was a silly-billy or maybe I was not, but I think that I was smart enough, so I went into the first house I was passing, and asked if they did not need a servant, or a factory worker or any worker at all. I said that I would be happy to get a job, and a caretaker told me that a Jew lived over there and that he needed a servant, but the servants could not bear to stay there for long, three, four months, and then they were quitting. But I said, never mind, I have no other options available, and I went to see the family, they were happy to offer me the job and I stayed in their place. They were of a higher class. I must have stayed there for three or even four years.*

Her employer was a rabbi. She worked for this family until the outbreak of WWII. She had a room for her disposal and rather 'gallant' wages. *I had very good conditions with this family. Initially they paid me 12 zloty per month, and then 25 zloty.* She spent the money exclusively to meet her own needs, on clothes in particular. She did not make any friends in Łódź, and kept away from big city life. She reports that *I was not really meeting* [with anyone] *because I was afraid of everything, I did not know who I was dealing with. I did not know the people, and my father always used to say, 'Remember one thing, if you do something wrong, I would carry you on a pitchfork to the middle of the street', and that was sufficient warning for me.*

On the day of the outbreak of the War, Leokadia returned to her family village. Together with her sister, she applied for work at a land property owned by a German, which was twenty kilometres away from the village, to avoid forced deportation to Germany. The farm must have been large, as it seasonally employed a large group of young Polish people. Leokadia remembers that 25 girls slept in a barrack. This is where she met Tadeusz, her husband, who lived in the labourers' quarters[1] with his parents. His father worked as a wheelwright on the farm. Leokadia married the young carter in 1940, and their first child was born a year later. The young couple moved into Tadeusz's parents' house, however soon afterwards, Tadeusz was deported to Germany, and Leokadia moved to another village to work as a servant for a German family to avoid forced labour in Germany. The mother-in-law looked after the child until the war ended, and Leokadia came back to the parents-in-law after the Poland's liberation. She bought a pregnant cow from Russian soldiers, paying for it with vodka and butter. The cow calved on the day of Tadeusz's return from Germany, in December 1945. Soon after his return, Tadeusz found a job as a wheelwright at a nearby farm and the family moved there. This is where Krystyna was born in 1946, however Leokadia decided that Łódź would provide better prospects. She sold the cow and the pig, and the family moved to Łódź. They rented a two-room apartment near Bałucki Market. It was not connected to water supply, sewerage, gas supply systems. They had to fetch water from the market. Later it was delivered in water wagons. But Leokadia was used to such living conditions in the countryside, and she liked the apartment. She also encouraged her brother and sister to come to Łódź. They moved into apartments in the same yard, and another brother lived with Leokadia's family until he found a separate apartment. She started to work as a ward attendant in a nearby hospital soon

---

1 The term 'labourers' quarters' refers to the buildings where workers employed in the land property lived.

after they moved to Łódź, and her husband started to work as a carpenter. She worked in hospitals for over twenty years. She mostly worked night shifts to harmonise her duties of the mother and the employee. She gave birth to two more children, however one died in infancy. She stopped procreating in 1951. This is how she describes her material situation: *We did not have too much, what else, but we did not go to bed hungry, and that was most important, not to go to bed hungry.* Krystyna is less reserved and this is how she views these aspects: *I had very good conditions at* [parent's] *home. Dad was hardworking, so was mum, hence we had enough food, and we never experienced hunger. We had everything at home.* They had meat every day. *A soup and a second course, we would always get two courses. We had everything, we bred pigs, a few hens, so we never lacked anything.* Leokadia was responsible for breeding the animals, which probably lived in a shed, while Tadeusz was going to another not registered job after he had returned from his main place of employment and had lunch. *He was either building houses, or fitting windows or floors* – Krystyna recollects. The family's financial status was so good that Leokadia and her husband bought a plot of land to build a house. When television sets were available, they were the first family in their tenement house to buy one. Both children and adults from the neighbourhood used to come to their apartment to watch television. However in the early 1960s Tadeusz became ill, which affected their plans to build their own house. Due to muscular atrophy he could only walk using crutches, and then he was diagnosed with cancer of the duodenum. Nevertheless, even the father's disease did not induce a crisis situation as Leokadia always knew how to manage available resources soundly. *We did not have major* [financial] *reserves. We always had some savings in case of an illness or an emergency, it was necessary... today I have a job, tomorrow I can become unemployed, which would leave me without any money. So I had to prevent this, and always had to have some money.* She was also saving money to organise weddings for her children. Her husband's illness made her search for options to change their apartment. The first apartment was situated in an area which is now a pocket of poverty. It was connected to the sewerage system in the 1950s, and was provided with gas and water supply systems. But it was on the second floor, which was a barrier to Tadeusz who had to support himself with two crutches, therefore his options for leaving home were limited. She received a new municipal apartment in a panel block in the late 1960s, where she continues to live. It is a small 35 metre one-bedroom apartment, with a kitchen and bathroom, on the first floor. Leokadia also found ways to work for a higher retirement pension. Her salary as a ward attendant was low, therefore her pension would also be low, so she quit the job in the hospital and started to work in a mail-order store, which she retired from in 1978. Her husband died in the same year. She remarried two years later, and the other husband died five years later. She has been a widow since then.

Her daughter Krystyna was born in 1946 in the village, but spent all her childhood in Łódź. She is one of Leokadia's three living children. She has an elder brother, who is a shoemaker, and a younger sister, who is a qualified cook. She completed elementary school, although had to repeat Year Five, and continued her education in a basic vocational school of clothing industry. She did not complete that school as according to Leokadia *she had to get married.* She got pregnant and had a daughter Katarzyna (1965), when she was nineteen. After the wedding the couple moved into Krystyna's parents' apartment. They divorced when the child was two, but none of the respondents told us why Krystyna divorced her first husband. Krystyna and Leokadia worked and the disabled grandfather took care of the child. When the parents received the apartment in the block, Krystyna, who was a single mother, received a very small municipal apartment composed of one room, located in an old part of Łódź. Then, most likely after her second marriage, she illegally occupied a one-room apartment in a building designated for demolition. When the demolition work was due to begin, she received a council two-bedroom apartment with a total space of 58 square metres, which had all the sanitary installations. At that time she already had at least two daughters with her second husband. She had three children, including Katarzyna, and pursuant to the housing regulations she was eligible to receive an apartment with sufficient space. In 1977, she had another daughter. Krystyna's second husband was an alcoholic. He would start arguments and used to beat her. The family had to go to his employer's on paydays to ensure that he did not go anywhere to spend all wage on alcohol. There is no information on the place of his employment. Krystyna does not mention her previous two marriages, and the daughter doesn't know which job her step-father did and where he worked. She only declares that *anyway, we always had enough food at home, I cannot complain. There was even a time when the* [step] *father used to work, as the girls were little, but we always had enough, there were no crisis situations.* But the reoccurring rows made Krystyna divorce her husband and have him evicted from the apartment. The[step] father's alcoholism most likely contributed to the fact that Krystyna's two daughters were unable to complete elementary school, and are graduates of a school for children with special needs. The third daughter born from this marriage only completed elementary school. In 1985 Krystyna remarried again. Her third husband, with whom she continues to live, was also born in 1965 and comes from a single-parent family. He completed elementary school, and at the time of their marriage, worked as a driver. About three years after the wedding he had an accident. He was crushed by a car, which resulted in damage to his chest, and had to have a lung removed. He contracted jaundice in the hospital, however he was ineligible for a disability pension as the medical committee decided that he was still fit to work. He cannot find any work. He only has one lung, and thus gets tired very quickly. He completed various courses organised by the Employment Office, attends job fairs, however he has not found any work, and has been unemployed for ten years.

Krystyna worked as a blue-collar worker for 15 years. First she was a ward attendant in the same hospital that used to employ her mother, then she was a cleaner in an asbestos factory; she has also been a rubbish sorter, and finally worked as a toilet lady in a public toilet. After the Municipal Sanitation Company, which managed public toilets, was privatised, and *people were made redundant*, Krystyna lost her job in the early 1990s, and has no perspectives on being re-employed. She has been suffering from anaemia for a long time, and a year ago she broke her hand and had to undergo complicated surgery. Her hand does not work properly and she is even unable to do some housework. Social assistance benefits are her source of income. Two years ago she moved out of her block to an old tenement house in a pocket of poverty, as she was unable to pay the rent on the previous apartment. Her current accommodation consists of two rooms, a kitchen, a landing and a bathroom, and has a total area of 62 square metres. An internal central gas heating system is used to warm the apartment. It is furnished with old types of furniture, which are however in good condition. When the husband was working *we managed somehow. Maybe we did not have any luxuries, but we had enough to pay the bills, and if we felt like having an ice-cream, it was affordable. And now we are deprived of everything. Our life is so hard that I feel like crying most of the time*. Krystyna cannot count on her children's help because *the children have their own life and problems, and their own children. Where are they going to get the money from to help me? They do not have the money anyway.* The mother-in-law sometimes *brings radishes, a piece of bread, a small bone* [to make a soup with] *and this helps us to survive.* Krystyna eats meat *when mum sometimes invites me for lunch ...* [*or*] *when mum gives me some minced meat, or something like that, and then we have it. And if they give me no meat, then we do not eat it.*

Katarzyna has replicated her mother's life history. She was brought up without a father, with the disabled grandfather sometimes being the father figure. After her mother remarried, Katarzyna lived with her and the step-father. When she was seven, her sister was born, and she reports that *from that moment the step-father started to reject me. Eighteen months later another sister was born. The youngest sister was born in 1977, and after that I never had a happy childhood. Only his daughters mattered, and I was least important.* She never deserved a word of praise from her mother's husband. *If he bought something, he gave it to the sisters, and not to me.* Presumably the step-father disliked his step-daughter because as the eldest daughter she defended her mother when he abused her in his alcoholic rages. *And he often beat me because of this,* she recollects. On his payday, Katarzyna's mother sent her to bring the father home to prevent him from going out drinking. In such situations, the grandparents used to take Katarzyna to their apartment. She lived with them in the block until she graduated from the elementary school, where she had learning difficulties. She had to repeat Year Five, just like her mother did. Grandmother convinced her to continue her education at a basic vocational school for the clothing industry. She used the argument that the girl was not doing well at school, and that in her opinion Katarzyna should have a sedentary job, as her hip had been broken as a result of a car accident when she was twelve. The school was near Katarzyna's mother's home and that is why she moved back to her mother and step-father's apartment. These events coincided with grandmother's wedding, therefore it is likely that Leokadia wanted to live only with her new husband and due to this, she sent her granddaughter back to her mother's. In the meantime Krystyna was trying to evict her husband from the apartment and needed Katarzyna to assist her with this. The step-father occupied one room while the other two were used by the mother and four girls. After Katarzyna completed the basic school she started to work as a nursery teacher's assistant because, as she says herself, she always liked children and wanted to work with them. The poor school results prevented her from *becoming a teacher.* When she was seventeen years old, she met her future husband, whom she married five years later. After their wedding reception, which was partly financed by the mother-in-law, who took a loan for this purpose, Katarzyna and her husband moved into her mother's apartment. At the time, Krystyna had had a new husband for about a year. They occupied one room, and Katarzyna and her family received the second, while the third room was at the disposal of the younger sisters. The young couple's first son was born after one year, and they lived at Krystyna's apartment for three years, probably until one of the sisters got married or had a baby, and had nowhere else to live. Katarzyna's family moved to her parents-in-law. It was a critical moment in her life, as it turned out that the father-in-law was an alcoholic, who had systematically got his son addicted to vodka. The respondent says that before she married, she did not know that her husband and father-in-law used to drink. That is how it was with her husband: *Boys will be boys, and sometimes he got drunk, but he did not drink all the time, not then.* His addiction became apparent after they married. He started coming back home late and kept saying that he had to stay longer at work. After a bout of drinking he would go to his parents, to stay the night at their place. When they had to move out from Katarzyna's mum's apartment to the parents-in-law's, the son and the father started drinking together. Katarzyna's husband quit his job at a state-owned enterprise and started working at a private company together with this father. He was a qualified cabinet-maker, however he re-qualified in order to do carpentry work. Katarzyna wanted to save her marriage and distract her husband from alcohol, so after Leokadia's second husband died, she moved with her family into the apartment of her grandmother, who detested alcohol. It was not much help as Katarzyna's husband kept drinking and making rows anyway. The respondent unexpectedly became pregnant again, and as she reports *everyone advised me not to have this baby, because they knew what he was like, and told me to have an adoption* [she means abortion]. *But I said that I would not murder my child.* The baby's birth did not change Katarzyna's husband's behaviour, and it is likely that Leokadia told him to move out of her apartment. He went back to his parents, and Katarzyna and her children stayed at grandmother's. However after six months he talked her into moving back into his parents' apartment. Despite his previous promises that he would stop drinking, he quickly fell back into the addiction and starting rows. Katarzyna took the children and moved back to her grandmother for good, and filed a divorce petition and an application for child maintenance. She has been divorced for three years. Her financial situation is very hard, and without Leokadia's help she would be unable to support herself and the children. She is jobless and ineligible to receive unemployment benefits. She was made redundant as the nursery in which she had worked was liquidated. She had registered as an unemployed person and was receiving unemployment benefit for over two years. Its amount was very low as the salary of a nursery teacher's assistant, which provided the basis to calculate the benefit, was low too. When she was no longer entitled to receive the benefit, she found an unregistered job in 'grey economy' in a sewing room. She has been working there as a wrapper for about four years, but only in the periods when the sewing room receives enough orders. Unfortunately three or four-month long 'order-free' seasons occur in this company, and then Katarzyna does not earn any money. If there is work, she receives a wage ranging from 600–800 zloty per month, for ten to fourteen hours of work per day. Katarzyna realises that this work is not included in the employment register that provides the basis to calculate the amount of retirement pension, however she accepts this *because this is typical nowadays, and I have to cope somehow to have a job and earn the money.* Her family income includes allimony that father pays for the children

(250 zloty a month), family allowance (60 zloty a month) and 120 zloty of social assistance benefit. Grandmother Leokadia receives retirement pension of 540 zloty, thus the income per person in their joint household is 340 zloty. The family would not be able to live on this amount, so Katarzyna's work in the 'grey economy' helps them to survive. Accommodation-related fees and charges exceed 300 zloty a month, and Leokadia also has to spend some of the money on medication. Occasionally she also has to help her daughter Krystyna.

Katarzyna is not only excluded from the market of legal and secure employment. She does not socialise. She recollects: *I had many friends here, and many in my mum's neighbourhood. Everything would be ok, if not these rows and abuse. It has also made me very nervous. I still feel shuttered.* She does not keep in touch with her step-sisters. Two of them are unemployed, and the third one, the one who completed elementary school, used to work as an assistant in a sewing room, and now she makes clothes at home, most likely working in the grey economy. This is how Katarzyna explains the lack of contact with her step-sisters: *everyone is busy in one way or another, busy with their lives. They are younger than me. They keep closer... anyway, if I say something, if I confide my difficulties, all the family know at once, because they see one another and keep saying things, often adding untrue information.* This young woman is also excluded from political life. This is how she arguments it: [Now] *I do not vote. I used to vote when Wałęsa was a candidate. I voted for Wałęsa. I have not voted since then, and I am not involved in politics anyway, because when I sometimes listen to the news, it's all bad. And our life is never good, and it is getting worse. They, I mean the ones who hold these high positions, are enjoying good lives, and they are fighting for these positions, and they push for them...Everyone only cares to get a good position to have money. And they do not care about poor people, about those who sometimes cannot even afford to buy bread, they are not interested in such things.*

There are no grounds to assume that Katarzyna's children will overcome this vicious circle of poverty in which the F. family lives. Ryszard, her eldest son, has already shared the fate of his aunts and learns in a school for children with special needs: *He is so distracted that occasionally he loses his memory. It seems that he knows all the letters, and then a moment comes when he does not remember.* The boy became this nervous because of the rows caused by his drunken father. He was also beaten, and his father tormented him by locking him in a room on his own. Katarzyna describes: *It happened that* [the husband] *hit* [the son], *but if I was there, I would not let him do it, I never let him raise his hand to hit the child. But sometimes, he grabbed him, or something... Well, sometimes he would charge into the apartment, and he was mad, and he would grab a belt and beat him, and I was unable* [to stop him doing that]. *But it happened once that he locked the child in a room. It often happened that as soon as he reached our apartment door he was ready to start a row. And that definitely affected the children, which is why* [Ryszard] *is nervous.*

Grandmother Leokadia is the only 'safe ground' in this family. She receives retirement pension for her work in a socialist enterprise. Neither her daughter Krystyna nor her granddaughter Katarzyna stands a chance of receiving a pension. If the grandmother dies, they will be left without the support she gives them now. We can expect that Katarzyna will not be able to afford pay the cost of accommodation, and just like her mother, she will have to move to a pocket of poverty. The fate of her other son is also predetermined. Katarzyna would like her younger son to become a physician, but she knows that *these might only be my dreams.*

The grandmother left the pocket of poverty, the daughter went back to it, and the granddaughter will definitely go back to it too.

2. The W. family

My parents could sleep soundly because they knew that whether I passed my exams or not I would have a job. I have three children and I can't sleep without a worry, like my father did. So I will bring them up and educate them – that means nothing. Nothing.

The W. Family is a 'Łódź' family of at least the fourth generation. The father of our interviewee, Wanda (born in 1931), who has grandchildren at the moment, was born in 1907 in Łódź. Her daughter Maria (born in 1954) is dependent on social welfare as well as assistance provided by her mother and other individuals. Maria is the first woman in the family who is impoverished, and is following a poor person's trajectory. Not only has she become significantly poorer, but she has also become socially degraded. She had to leave her cooperative flat in a multi-storey building on a newly-built housing estate and move to an old tenement house in a substandard part of the city. Since she hasn't been paying the electricity bill in her new place, she had electricity in the flat cut off and therefore no heating. She graduated from secondary school – a construction technical school – and was initially employed by a renowned planning and design company, whereas her last job was that of a cleaner in a school. Her first husband graduated from secondary school and her second husband has primary education. They are currently separated although they share the same flat.

Before the War, Maria's grandparents (Wanda's parents) – Kazimierz and Marianna – were employed in a factory that produced lingerie, and lived on the factory's premises. Thus, they belonged to a not too-numerous category of workers with a secure material situation. But the war caused transient poverty in the family. In 1942, Maria's grandfather was deported to forced labour in Germany and Maria's grandmother was the only breadwinner for a family with three young children, one of whom was born during his absence. In 1943, the family was forced to leave the flat they had occupied until then. Marianna had to move in with her mother and sister. Wanda was the eldest of her children – being twelve years-old at the time – she took care of her younger siblings and ran the household. This was a traumatic period in her life, although thanks to the protection of a German woman whose place they occupied at the time, she was not deported to forced labour in Germany, which happened to many of her peers: *The hostess of the house* [where the interviewee lived] *was a German and two of her daughters lived there. And this was Mrs K. – I don't remember her name – but she was so kind, she was helpful to everyone. I might have been sent to Germany to forced labour so I don't know where I would have ended up were it not for her. She issued a statement that I was helping her, being 12, 13 and 14 at the time that my father was deported to Germany and that my mother was with three of her children and that I was taking care of those children and that I was helping her and others when they needed it.*

They were not starving at the time *thanks to that German lady* [since] *there was her bakery in their yard, so they had enough dry bread whenever they wanted.* The basic food of Wanda and her brother *was half a pot of turnip, (and) it was great whenever there were some potatoes. Potatoes covered by this black oatmeal. Topped with margarine.* She would cook milk soup for her youngest sister from milk allocated to all of the children. Hence, Wanda is weeping: *I wouldn't taste milk* [*since*] *our portion of milk, skimmed milk anyway, was given to the smallest child.*

The Nazi-German occupation was decisive to her fate. It interrupted her education at school. After the war, she graduated from primary school in an accelerated mode (she did three school years in a year and a half). Having graduated from primary school, she was admitted to the second year of secondary school. *However, I had to do history on my own. That is, not together with all other students of the same grade. Well, I failed since my mum went to hospital in May and I went to hospital after her. Mum had heart problems and I had my appendix removed afterwards. Once out of hospital, and this went on for some time, I couldn't catch up. I didn't make up for wasted time at school.* In 1949, she started work as a forewoman in a winding department. She met her future husband there. He worked at the same plant in the sourcing department. *All young people* [at the plant] *were organised in all sorts of choirs, we went to the ballet, other events, different meetings let's say, and this is how we met* – Wanda recalls. They had a civil wedding ceremony in 1951 and a church wedding before the First Communion of their eldest daughter. Their first daughter – our main interviewee Maria – was born in 1954. Her sister Ewa was born five years later.

Wanda and Tadeusz are still married. They formed a typical Łódź worker family that devoted all their efforts to ensuring a better life for their daughters. They worked until retirement. Both daughters graduated from secondary school. They wanted to gain a higher education, but didn't pass the entrance exams: Maria wanted to study civil engineering at the Łódź Technical University, whereas Ewa wanted to study law at the University of Łódź. Ewa is married. She has one daughter. She has worked in the Dean's office of a university from the moment she received her secondary school diploma. According to her mother, her husband *is a very well-behaved man, a really cultured person and from a very respectful family.*

Maria is in a totally different situation, although there were no signs that she would become a welfare beneficiary. Maria had no problems completing primary school, and following the advice of her father, who worked as an interior decorator in a renovation and construction cooperative, she went to secondary technical school for construction. She had to do the first year twice because of difficulties with mathematics, but she did the rest without problems. She was even a student board chairwoman. She describes her parents' home as a 'normal home' where *I was never hungry, first of all, I was never short of bread, butter or warmth.* Her mother states that *we did our best so that they* [their daughters] *would have a bun for school, so that they would be dressed in such a way that they're happy and they remember it really until now, and they do remember, and they praise us that they started each school year wearing new shoes, with new uniforms and having new books.* Maria spent summer holidays with her grandparents. She went to a summer youth camp only once. She did not want to repeat the experience as she returned with lice after her first youth camp. While at secondary technical school, she regularly participated in summer camps organised by the Socialist Youth Union. In 1975, shortly after graduating from secondary school, she began working at a design company in Łódź. She decided to undertake work and not study at the university full time, since, as she puts it, *I was fed up of hearing that I owed everything to him* [father]. *So I'm saying 'Oh no. Enough is enough. I want to stand on my own two feet'. And I was! I was! I took up work which I had found myself.* However, she took the entrance exams for working students to the university, but failed. She tried again two years later, and failed again. Her striving for independence from her father was so strong that she pursued caring for an elderly person in exchange for accommodation. When she started earning better money she wanted to rent a flat, but her father decided that she could leave their family home only as a married woman. She recalls: *I was working in a design office and so I could afford to rent a flat, but my father told me he wouldn't let me go while I was carrying his surname. Such a traditionalist he* [was].

The girl soon began to succeed at work. *Four months later my boss decided to promote* [me]. *This is how you become a drafter, an assistant. Hassle, as you would say today. How come, after four months? You have to work for at least two years to do that. No, 'She's talented' my manager said, and he disregarded that aspect of it. Then there was a shock again, since I hadn't worked for even a year and I was promoted to the post of Senior Assistant.* In the interviewee's opinion, this caused envy among her colleagues, the majority of whom were also from her school (the design company was the school's patron). *They would draw on me and behave nastily, really nastily. There were, for example, unpleasant things on a daily basis. It was disgusting. I didn't take up this job to feel as I don't know who. I was in an architectural department at some point for 5 years, and then I moved to a construction department. And I made a mistake in that, because it was even worse there in terms of male-female relations and I resigned of my own volition.*

In 1978, while still working at the design company, Maria got married to Arek, who was working at the same company as an assistant designer. She moved out of her family home into a rented flat after the wedding. According to her, this marriage was a mistake. *I mean* – she says – *that when I was getting married to him I was aware that I was lying to him, since I didn't love him. But he believed he had enough love for the two of us.* Presumably Maria came to the following conclusion after a miscarriage. *Since we didn't have the baby, none of it made sense. I can't go on like this any longer. How can you lie to yourself and to him? How long can you do it? Enough time has passed.*

She called a taxi, packed her things and returned to her parents. However, it turned out that *there was no space for me in my sister's room, which I used to share with her. My things had to hang everywhere, on door handles, on windows, on something else, as there was no space for them in the closet, and I was getting in the way... This was an unpleasant experience since I was still working at the time, I would go on business trips and I was under control: where do I travel and what do I do and where do I go? And my father felt stupid. How come? She just got married and now I'm coming back home by car, by taxi, out of thin air.*

After her wedding, Maria did not de-register from her parents' place. After getting married, she applied to the municipal department of housing issues for temporary accommodation for a young couple. She was a member of a housing cooperative then, and she was entitled to temporary accommodation while waiting for a cooperative flat. She, her parents and her father's brother all chipped in to make a contribution to the housing cooperative. She then had to wait for a long time to receive the flat. Unexpectedly, she received temporary accommodation shortly after having moved in with her parents – it turned out that one of the tenants in the tenement house where her parents lived was moving out. Maria applied for that flat and got it, although she had some difficulties with the fact that she was not yet divorced at that time. It was a twenty-three-square-meter room, with the sink in the corridor and the toilet in the yard. There was no gas. The flat was renovated by her father. But Maria still did not get on well with him, since *he was simply ashamed. What was he supposed to tell neighbours* [that I lived there alone]*? And what he came up with was that he* [Maria's husband] *had gone abroad to make money and I got the flat. That we just got that flat. That we had been renting and we now had temporary accommodation and were waiting for the cooperative flat next. The situation became problematic when people started visiting me at my flat. My* [later, second] *husband, among others. How come? How can it be? Her husband is abroad and some chaps are visiting her.* The interviewee's father believed that his daughter had disgraced the family, broken existing norms and was immoral. Despite her father's objections, Maria registered her current husband in this flat before their wedding in September 1981. She got married to him a few months later. They share the place then, but they are separated now. Maria does not want to say much about him. We only know that he is four years younger than her and that he started technical school for motor vehicle engineering after having completed primary school. However, he did not even finish the first year as he had an accident and had to wear a cast. Maria's mother blames him for her daughter's bad financial situation. Wanda says: *Frankly speaking, the fact of the matter is that my son-in-law did not take care of things. He didn't work, didn't earn money… I've known him for more than fifteen years and this is what I can tell you, that during those fifteen years he hasn't worked long enough to have a paid, decent holiday. He is a rolling stone. Barely half a year passes between his first job and the next one. Whenever a child was born, he wouldn't be working at the time, he wouldn't have regular income and whenever he had some income he would only get one tenth of the money.* However, Maria seemed to be enchanted by him since she decided to share a flat with him, and later on marry him after a short period of acquaintance.

Maria also started having problems at work. She does not want to or is unable to present the history of her employment. Therefore, we cannot determine her overall work experience. As stems from her chaotic statements, following her resignation from the design company, she found employment in a school dormitory where she was in charge of invoices. As she puts it: *I didn't like the relations there either. In fact they* [the bosses] *made me leave. However, I could sense that I simply didn't fit in with these women.* Later on, she undertook employment in a housing cooperative, where her father worked. As she says, *I was a senior inspector. Next to the director… I was calculating, all the invoices were checked and signed by me. I was next only to the director. Well, unfortunately I got sick. I got a facial palsy and I was threatened by paralysis.* She was given a 6-month sick leave. However, she returned to work a month later and continued treatment. She went to massages for two months. *I even had strychnine injections to get back on my feet.* While she was on sick leave, someone broke into her desk. *It turned out* – she recalls – *that my calculator was used, my desk was opened, my stamps were used and some timber was gone. I learned about that, I saw those signatures and I saw who it was and what it was. You know what, these were people who* [had worked] *for 2, 3, 5 years and not these busters, pardon me, in for apprenticeships or something, or school graduates – these were more experienced employees. They had the courage to put their signatures. And what am I supposed to do? To put them behind bars? I didn't resign. I simply left. Unauthorised departure from the workplace. I came to work, I signed an invoice and that was it. And I simply didn't go to work the next day. My father was terribly upset. That I had brought disgrace on him. He was all nerves. Time passed and he learned about it.* Presumably, the embezzlement (of several thousand, according to Maria) was somehow hushed up, since Maria does not mention the fact that somebody was sued. However, as she puts it, *she has negative references*, as it was *considered workplace abandonment.*

Her next job was again that of an employee in a design office. Because of the previous workplace abandonment issue, she received the lowest remuneration for three months and her employer was a little suspicious of her. She was employed there in 1983, when pregnant with her first child. In 1984, she gave birth to a son, Tomasz. Tomasz was frequently ill, and so did not qualify for a nursery as he required constant care. Maria then decided to go on a two-year childcare leave. Two years later, she wanted to return to work but her son was still not well enough for a nursery. She therefore applied for an extension of her childcare leave, but as she puts it, the director *didn't want to give me a third year off, as I should have informed him 3 or 4 days earlier. However, how could I have guessed that there would be such a situation, that my child would require such care. Anyway, my superior told me 'You know what, you have such problems with your child', and he set a condition: 'Either you resign yourself, or we're going to dismiss you'. 'You must be joking', I told him. I wouldn't give them that satisfaction and I resigned of my own volition. Thank you. Good-bye. And then there was nothing. No job whatsoever.*

We can guess that the director made use of a formal pretext to exclude Maria from his team. From the point of view of her employer, Maria abused the right that working women were entitled to in the days of Socialism. She started work pregnant, and then used sick leave during her pregnancy, and subsequently went on childcare leave. She was occupying a position that could be given to someone else. Since teams in design offices were remunerated based on their performance, the lack of a drafter created difficulties for the designers and diminished the wages of all the employees in a given department. The director might have sensed that Maria was pregnant again. And that was true. Had he not forced her to resign, he would not have had a drafter for four more years.

That Maria was consciously using tactics of undertaking permanent employment while being pregnant cannot be ruled out, since she undertook her latest employment as a cleaner at school in 1992 while again pregnant.

As stems from her recollections, she found herself in a critical situation in 1986. *Too much pressure* – she recalls – *A baby, pregnancy, my husband on his business trips and I was with that baby. I wouldn't have gone along if I had been working… It all happened simultaneously… And I said one thing to my husband. I told him I was going to abort this second baby, this was a way out, and I go to work then and I wouldn't have* [childcare leaves] *but I would earn what was needed and I would afford to hire someone.* Her husband did not agree to the abortion. Ania was born in 1987.

While taking care of her children, Maria tried to become a sole proprietor. As we can guess, she tried to offer drafter's services on commission. She thought it would be a bull's eye, since she used to get lots of offers for commissioned tasks while working at the design office. She registered her entrepreneurial activity with the Municipal Office and made announcements in the newspapers. But, it was a failure. Maria had purchased a drawing board and rapidographs to do drawings in accordance with her experience, but it was in vain as no designer was interested in commissioning work to her. Perhaps this happened because design offices were in big trouble at the time. They weren't getting the orders themselves. This might have happened because computers replaced drawing boards at the time. Thus, Maria's skills might have been insufficient.

Although her entrepreneurial activity had failed, our interviewee experienced great joy in 1989: she received a cooperative flat in a new housing estate. She had been waiting for it for fifteen years. This was a three-room flat with two hallways, a kitchen, bathroom and a toilet. This was a huge improvement in the housing conditions of Maria's family, who had so far been squatting in a twenty-three-square-meter flat with no toilet, running water or gas. It was presumably in their new place of residence that serious problems began in her family. Maria's youngest daughter Magdalena was part of these problems. Frankly speaking, neither Maria nor her mother Wanda wanted to speak about the situation. According to Maria, her husband Wojciech had previously been a good father: *When I gave birth to our son* – she recalls – *he was happy, he was on cloud nine. There was a crate of champagne waiting and many other things, you name it. We didn't have an automatic washing machine, we only had running water and a tub. It was terribly hot and my husband was wringing out nappies, drenching and wringing out them and then drenching again so the baby could breathe.* However, he later questioned the paternity of his youngest daughter. Maria claims there are no grounds for this doubt. The only explanation she has is that she herself realised it very late that she was pregnant. Her local physician convinced her that her irregular menstrual cycle was associated with menopause. It was only when she went to a paid private physician that she learned that she was five months pregnant. Maria says: *I didn't do anything wrong. Only that doctor kept me unaware of the situation for so long. How was I supposed to inform others about it? I'm five months pregnant! You couldn't tell from looking at me. Not at all!* And then, *I was aware that my husband claimed that she wasn't his child. And I'm saying, 'I shit you not', pardon me. 'I know she is your child. You will grow to understand it'. No, I won't do harm to her. Even if I had 600 zloty, or whatever in order to do it [an abortion], I won't do it since I won't risk making two children orphans. I'm not that dumb. Really, believe me. I'm not that stupid. Even if I were cursed, even if everyone turned away from me, I wouldn't have left this child. I wouldn't be able to do that.* She gave birth to Magda in the 29th week of pregnancy via Caesarean section. This is how she presents her experience after childbirth: *I woke up with problems, as it was a few hours later than expected. I needed a blood transfusion but I refused, because of AIDS and whatever. I didn't have contact with my husband. I felt so lonely then.* It seems that this situation persists to this day. Maria does not want to tell us about her husband and her marriage. She claims that *there were no misunderstandings but there was no understanding, either.* She does not trust her husband, although they have been married for sixteen years. We do not know exactly what Wojciech does. He is probably a driver travelling long distances. Our interviewee even mentions that he took their son with him while travelling abroad.

Having lived in a block of flats for seven years, their debts were so large that Maria had to move into an old tenement house. It usually happens that a new buyer pays the debts in a housing cooperative and gives some money 'privately' to the family that's moving out. Maria and her children and husband moved to a part of the city currently inhabited by a large number of people living on welfare, that is, to a pocket of poverty. By a stroke of bad luck she now resides on the same street her grandparents used to live on, and where her mother was born, although in those days it was not a pocket of poverty. Her current flat is approximately 60 square meters, with two rooms and a kitchen. There is no bathroom, but there is a toilet. When the family moved in, the apartment was electrically heated, *however, a sad thing happened. I can't afford heating so it was switched off. Electricians came, these gentlemen came and switched off the heating because we couldn't afford the heating. However, I have a coal stove, a beautiful one, a very nice one, a brown one.* Maria wept as she told us about her *terrible financial problems. At some point I couldn't organise Christmas. I went to my parents. It wasn't for me – although I also missed doing it – but my children needed to see it* [a real Christmas]. She would not be able to survive at all without the help of her parents and other relatives. Her parents primarily take care of Maria's son. *Tomek comes here every Friday after classes* – Wanda told us – *and this is how it is. He arrives on Friday and I bring him back home on Sunday evening. One mouth less to feed at my daughter's. When we need to buy him a winter jacket, we have been buying it for fourteen years already. And you need to buy him, let's say, two pairs of shoes a year. And when he goes to school in September you have to buy him things. He receives rucksacks from his grandparents, shoes from his grandparents and jackets from his grandparents.* Grandma takes care of the boy when he makes efforts to earn money on his own. [Tomek] *was distributing leaflets before the election. I assisted him just a little because the neighbourhood was unfamiliar to him. I didn't want him to suffer any harm. He was distributing leaflets and earned seventy zloty. Grandpa added fifteen zloty and he bought a winter jacket.* Ania and Magda also receive clothes from their relatives. However, these are mainly used clothes. *So Tomasz's sister Ania, the middle child so to speak, gets a lot of things from P. – shoes, jackets, sweaters and even some underwear like pyjamas and things like that. And her aunt will always buy her something, too. Magda, on the other hand, was* [born] *after my sister's* [granddaughter]. [My sister's] *daughter lives in Łódź and* [her daughter] *is a year older than Magda, the smallest one. So they are really not in need when it comes to clothes. Clothes are passed on to them and they have good stuff. Not worn out. Ania also got a lot of sweaters and dresses – very tidy, beautifully packed – from her friend recently,* Wanda said.

The need to help Maria caused tensions and conflicts in her parents' marriage. They are so serious that each of them now has their own money. *There were unpleasant incidents, not violence God forbid, but very unpleasant conversations that I was wasting money on the eldest daughter and providing for my son-in-law, a lazybones.* [My husband] *always hassled me before he got cash – this and that – so I made the decision, since I was already mentally and nervously exhausted, and I said 'You're going to have your money and I'm going to keep my money'* Wanda told us, embarrassed. Since her pension is very small (450 zloty per month), she receives an annual allowance from her last workplace. And also *I have an elderly aunt. She is 86. I will cook for her, bring it to her. I can't say that I'm using her. But the thing is that the money she gives me for her food, we cook this pot of food and share it between us and this is how we get along.*

Living in a pocket of poverty also means new neighbours and finding oneself in a dysfunctional environment. Maria still believes that she is better-off than her neighbours as she has different habits (she does not borrow personal items from others), and resources (towels, underwear). She is irritated by the fact that her neighbour wanted to bury her husband in a borrowed suit, since he did not have his own. She does not acknowledge the fact that her children are already wearing clothes, including personal items, already worn by other children, not necessarily relatives. Our interviewee is concerned about the future of her children. She says: *I have three children and I know nothing about what will become of them. About their future. I can't sleep soundly like my father did…* [since] *my father and mother knew that whether I passed the exams or not, I would have a job. And I will raise, I will educate my children and what will come of it? And what will they do next?*

It seems that Maria has well-grounded concerns about the future of her children, although she still believes that they will be able to acquire a good education. She is afraid that they will find it difficult to find employment, despite education. Meanwhile, younger daughters have rather poor chances of receiving a good education. Tomek can still get help from his grandparents. After their death, Maria will only get help from welfare institutions. There is no hope that she can get employment in line with her profession. Her qualifications are useless now, as design work has changed. It would be great if she could find a full-time job as a cleaner. However, even if she starts such work immediately, she will still be short several years of the seniority required to receive a retirement pension. Thus, there are reasonable grounds to predict that living conditions for Maria and her children will deteriorate rather than improve. Maria is on a downward trajectory due to a combination of circumstances related to the country's socio-political transformation (changes in the labour market, an increase in bills and housing fees), and personal circumstances (multi-child family, disintegration of her marriage).

3. The Z. B. family

'*I worked for over fifty years, without a break, and today I have a four hundred zloty* [retirement pension].' (Maria)

'*It seems to me really that it used to be different, that you were respected by everybody, and now it is horrible. People are not so satisfied with their lives. It is true, there is no work, so we carry on poorly*' (Hanna).

The Z. B. family have had Łódź roots for at least three generations. Maria (born in 1926), its founder, was born in Łódź. Currently only Maria receives a regular and systematic but very low income. Two of her children and an adult granddaughter live on social security benefits.

Maria was born in a working class family, which consisted of father, mother and two children. That was an unusual situation as at that time Łódź families usually had several children. Nevertheless Maria's family had to receive assistance under the social security scheme. Maria's father first worked at a sewerage company, and when he became ill with arthritis and was unable to work, he did seasonal cleaning jobs at Źródliska Park. In winter he was receiving social benefits. Maria remembers that *I used to go to get this benefit with mum, I was a little girl then, and I used to go to Matejki Street... this is where people were receiving the benefits, which reminded the current unemployment benefit. And that was a standard until the war. Our life was hard when dad did not work, and then mum used to get a home-based job from Jews who managed such home-based businesses, and they were making scarves, and we were crocheting fringes and then attached them to the scarves, and they paid us for this job, so that is how we could earn extra money, mum earned extra money in this way.*

Maria went to school and did her homework using light from an oil lamp, as Bałuty [district] was not connected to power grid before the war. She had managed to complete the fifth year at school before the war started, and she did not continue education after the war. The situation of Maria's parents was very difficult, although Maria herself did not experience poverty. Her aunt and uncle were a wealthy family and had no children. They provided most of funds to raise her. In fact they performed the function of Maria's foster family: *Mum's sister was a widow and she married a very wealthy bloke, they married at a rather old age, and this step uncle had a private business, he worked, and had a shop and an upholstery workshop. He was very wealthy and they helped my parents a lot, they took me to their apartment and raised me, i.e. they did not adopt me, I simply lived at their apartment, went to a local school in their area, the uncle was buying clothes for me, he sent me to the first communion, i.e. he bought everything that I needed, and later sent me to a summer camp or took me to the countryside, and I was travelling with this uncle, and he paid for my wedding.*

Maria's parents lived in a district that Germans intended to turn into a Jewish ghetto thus in December 1940 they received an order to vacate their apartment. After a short time of living in a rented room they moved to an apartment in which Maria lived until 1962. In June 1941, she was made to go to Germany for forced labour. She came back home in February 1945, and already at the beginning of March she took up a job at a small sewing company, which was later merged with Lido company. Maria worked there for twenty seven years, and this is where she met her husband. He also was a blue-collar worker at the same factory. Her parents were dead by then thus the uncle who had raised Maria sponsored her wedding. *And after the wedding, when my husband joined the army, he promised that he would sponsor my lunches for a year, until my husband's return, and even when I was going to see my husband, my uncle always paid the cost, gave me money when I did not have enough to pay for a trip or buy some cold meats or something to take for my husband. I was lucky to have him.* Maria got married in 1947, but had children after the husband returned from the army. The first son was born in 1951, a year later she had a daughter - Hanna, next she had another daughter in 1955, and a son in 1959. The whole family lived in a one-room apartment in which Maria's parents used to live. The apartment had no sanitary infrastructure. Maria did not stop working after she had had children. Her mother-in-law was a great help to Maria as she helped her to raise the children and run the household. This respondent could not rely on her husband as he *enjoyed drinking. He did not drink every day. He drank a little bit, not all the time, however it happened quite often.* Maria's mother-in-law took two oldest children to live with her, although her living conditions were very hard (one room without any amenities). The children stayed there until they went to school. Later on she was travelling from Chojny to Radogoszcz every day at 6 a.m. to enable Maria to go to work. Then after her husband's death, she moved into Maria's, who received an apartment in a block and continued to maintain household and raise children. Apart from working at the factory Maria also did cleaning and cooking jobs at wealthier families: *usually after work, after I left the sewing room, or on the days when I worked from 2 to 10, I used to go there in the morning. I had to vacuum clean the apartment, tidy it, wash up tea or coffee cups, and sometimes I would cook lunch for her, but all the food had to be very light as they suffered from liver problems, they did not use cream, no such additives, and she did the cooking herself really and I only did shopping on a market or at a greengrocer's, a little bit of vegetable, spuds, potatoes, and cabbage. I worked for her for about two years, and she was paying me, she always remunerated me, because she was very fond of me, because she kept everything at home and she would never lock anything when I was there, fur coats in a wardrobe, gold and other stuff, these people really trusted me. And then at Christmas she would buy something for me, a piece of fabric for a dress, or something else, maybe some food, and this is how I coped. This is how I coped.* Later the respondent did similar jobs at two other families. She also offered her services to wash up dishes during parties and wedding receptions. This is what Hanna, Maria's daughter, says when she recollects childhood *We were poor, but* [parents] *coped. Really well, because we could afford bread with butter or margarine, i.e. only basic foods, however our clothes were nicely washed, we were not hungry, and mum married us all off, that is how she used to be like.*

Finally, after fifteen years of trying, Maria received an apartment in a block, three rooms and a kitchen. The mother-in-law let her apartment out to tenants, and moved to Maria's, where she occupied one room, while Maria, her husband and the children, the remaining two. It significantly improved their housing conditions, although seven persons lived in that apartment. In 1972, Maria's husband had a heart attack and became a disability pensioner. He died in 1982 as a result of the fourth heart attack. The respondent has been a widow since then.

In 1974, Maria quitted her job at the sewing company and became a janitor at one of Łódź universities, hoping for a better pay. She worked there until 1992. She was entitled to claim the retirement pension earlier, however she decided to keep the job as her living standard was low. She worked for over fifty years, including the forced labour in Germany, she was hardly ever sick and never used any sick leaves. She liked her work, however she had serious family problems, initially with the husband who abused alcohol and then became chronically ill, and later, with her children. They all completed only elementary schools, but two eldest children had good jobs: a son worked as a baker and a daughter was a seamstress. A son and two daughters got married before their father's death. Maria reports: *I got severely indebted due to the weddings, but I kept taking loans and used other means, the cost was not so high then.* A year after Maria's husband death she had to swap the apartment in a block into an apartment in an old tenement house, which was at the edge of a today's pocket of poverty. It was not due to financial problems but due to family misunderstandings, as [each child, after the wedding] *wanted to* [live] *with mummy, this one wanted with mummy and the other one wanted too, everyone wanted to live in the block of flats because of the standard.* The apartments were swapped under the following terms: *this lady paid me the difference and left 20 metres of coals, she organised the removal.* Probably Maria distributed the money among her children. The apartment which she currently shares with her youngest, thirty-seven-year-old son, is on the fourth floor, and consists of a room, a kitchen, a bathroom and a toilet. It is heated with coal, which is a serious drawback. Maria has had a serious back problem and has not left the apartment for some time now, as walking up to the fourth floor is a major problem to her.

All Maria's children got divorced, and the eldest son died in her apartment several years ago. *I am so stressed* – she reports - *that all my three children got divorced after 10 years. The first son got divorced and so did the first daughter. The elder daughter had a good husband, he completed a secondary technical school and became a cook, now he is a chef, and he was working and earning money, but he wanted to go to Russia as Poles could go to work there, so he left. When he was gone, she stayed with a child and she was also pregnant with another. As soon as she felt that there was no control, as her husband was not there, she started drinking, and she had companions. When she gave birth, her other child was one year old and it kept being ill all the time, and had to stay in a hospital about 15 times. I have all the documentation. I took the child away from her as I was very sorry for him. I took him to my place to raise him, he is 16 years old now and still lives with me. He is a very good pupil and has 'A's in all subjects. So I live with this child and with my son. When the elder son got divorced, he had one* [a companion], *who was a lousy housewife, and she only kept stealing his money. He was a baker so his salary was very good, he used to work nights, while she was partying, and did other things too. So he moved into my apartment when she left him. She found another lover, and my son suddenly died at my apartment... And now one daughter leads a more or less decent life, she also got divorced, she raises children, and this elder granddaughter is here, with my grandson, and the other daughter* [disappeared] *without trace. Sometimes I see her, once every six months, once every three months. I am not really interested in her life...* [She] *also hardly ever comes to see me. She also has a partner, and that is how it is with her. And the son who lives with me is a 37 years old bachelor. So I live with this son and raise my grandson.* Maria became the foster mother of her grandson in 1983. *He was born in 1981... in 1982 or maybe in 83 I filed an application to the court because I had no money for this child. I received some money from social security for this child, but they gave me very little, 200 [zloty], 300, it was in the 1980s, it was very hard, and someone told me to go to a social security office, and that I have to register there. So I went there, and there was a lady, a guardian, and she told me that I had to file an application to become the boy's foster family and then I would receive the money for him, and that this would provide a basis for me to become his foster family, so I had to submit this application. My son-in-law came to the hearing, so did my daughter, but they reached a consensus as there were two children, and the son-in-law took one child, and my daughter took the other. I took the child and later applied to become foster family and since then I have been raising this child, he has been staying with me since 1983, after my husband died.*

Maria's financial situation is very difficult. She receives a very small pension of up to 410 zloty per month. The son who lives with her receives a social security benefit reaching 170 zloty. Maria reports that *he used to work at hospital emergency departments as an oxygen tank operator, and now there is no work for him, he has been unemployed for several years... Now he has completed* [a course] *for cutters, for seamstress, at the labour office, but there is no work for him.* Reports by all members of the family indicate that the son's help at home is genuinely wanted. He runs home of his mother who has become unwell since her eldest son died, does Hanna's, his sister's, laundry as she has no running water in her apartment. He also cares for Hanna's daughter and helps her with homework since the girl had to leave her family home due to roars. He also cares for the nephew who lives with him and his mum.

When Maria talks about the daughter who *leads a more or less decent life*, she means Hanna, a forty-three-year-old woman who has been unemployed for several years. Hanna's financial and housing status is dramatically bad. She completed elementary school without any problems, and then worked for a gardener to earn some money. Next she completed a company-affiliated vocational school and became a seamstress specialising in knitwear. She got married in 1976, after a brief dating period, as she *got pregnant with a daughter.* Parents held Hanna's wedding and gave her chairs, a coffee table and bedding as the wedding presents. *Later* – Hanna reports – *we incurred a credit for young couples, and bought children's furniture, living room furniture, a sofa and armchairs, and kitchen furniture.* The young couple with a baby lived in the city outskirts, in dreadful conditions. This is how daughter Barbara describes it: *we lived in a basement, this is how I can call this place I think, everything was falling apart, slugs, the type without a shell, were walking on the walls, mice were at home and rats in cellars, it was like in a countryside, a shit next to another shit.* Hanna also observes positive aspects of living in that part of the city as *there was fresh milk from cows, and this child, Basia, was growing well. There was a garden, and there were no cars so we did not have to mind the child continuously, only that apartment was so dreadful.* The family were unsuccessful in receiving another apartment, so they decided to demolish the premises completely to make it uninhabitable. This is what they did: *There was a chimney on the roof, and we knocked the chimney down to make a hole in the roof. When the chimney fell down, a hole formed in the kitchen ceiling. I had glasses, and a lamp shade there, and I left everything unchanged to convince them that the damage had not been intentional.* [My husband and brother] *collapsed that roof. Fire brigade came. And I had a small child, so we could not stay without the roof, and only then they granted me this apartment at Wieniawskiego Street. And when I saw that apartment, I said to myself, well, well, it is a villa.* The 'Villa' mentioned by Hanna consists of a room and a kitchen, and is located in a small tenement house in a pocket of poverty. It has no amenities, toilet ('a privy') is outside, in the yard, and tenants have to fetch water from the street. A street hydrant freezes in winter, and you *have to walk a long way to fetch water*. Apartments are very cold.

Before the wedding Hanna worked as a seamstress in the same plant that her mum used to work, and later, as a cleaner at a company which manufactured prefabricated building materials. After she gave birth to her first child she had to take a parental leave as Basia had to have a leg in plaster for two years, and then in a traction splint. Her husband, who was a blue collar worker in the same plant of prefabricated materials, already had a drinking problem, however he was not aggressive at the time. Roars started later, and in Hanna's opinion, his companions contributed to this. The drinking bouts lasted until late night hours, and after that, he was beating Hanna. Barbara reports: *When my father had too much to drink, and he often did that, he was going nuts, he was fabricating arguments and then all of a sudden he was going after mum with his fists and beat her without any reason. Sometimes we had to escape through a window, he poured boiling water at me as he took me for mum, so he filled a saucepan with boiling water and then poured it at me. He was so bad that there were several police interventions.*

Despite this situation Hanna decided to have another child, hoping that this would help him to give up vodka, but she was wrong. Roars and battering continued. Upon her friends and brother's advice, she filed a divorce petition. During the first hearing the court ordered separation: husband was to move to the kitchen, and Hanna with the children were to stay in the room. She had to have the door between the kitchen and the room bricked up as he was trying to kill her with an axe. She suspects that he put her room on fire, but as she reports *I did not call for the fire brigade because there are fake connections to electricity in this apartment* {it is not connected to the meter to avoid paying}, *so I was afraid.* The husband was evicted after the divorce and now Hanna lives with a fourteen-year-old daughter, who learns in a school for children with special needs. Hanna has been unemployed for five years and has no hope that she will ever find a job. She is a seamstress, which is a job that until recently was in demand in Lodz, however now employers consider her too old. She receives a special purpose benefit from the social security to pay for school lunches for her daughter. The girl also gets a teatime meal in a community centre run by nuns. The father has been ordered to pay 50 zloty maintenance for the younger daughter, however recently he has been unemployed and has no money to pay. This is how Hanna characterises her financial status: *I fall behind with electricity bills, I fall behind with paying rent, I have several debts. There are always debts and debts, and I cannot handle this. I* [borrow] *from one neighbour or from another, I pay back a debt to one neighbour and go to another to ask for a new loan. I burn old slippers, old clothes, something like this, in our fireplace. I cut some wood, so if it gets very cold, I make fire in this fireplace.* No relative can help Hanna as they are also poor. Her mother offers her a plate of soup when Hanna visits her. The woman would love to go to work as she is very worried *that if they discover her rent arrears,* [then] *they will evict her from this apartment.* Unregistered work at a gardener's is her last resort, however there are many candidates for this job. Hanna complains: *They do not want to employ me privately at the sewing company, as a cleaner, or at least to make buttons or do ironing. I used to be a cleaner in an office, and now cleaners hang on to this job, these women hang on to this job, as it is hard to find a job like this anywhere now. And if you would like to work somewhere else, in a better office, now there are such brigades, and a private businessman hires cleaners and manages them, he has his own people, who go there and do the cleaning.* Her private life after the divorce has improved significantly, although she still has not fully recovered. For the past five years she has had an informal relationship with a man who *also helps me, helps me a lot, whenever he can* – she declares. They live separately, as he takes care of his mother, who has schizophrenia. Hanna goes to their apartment, bathes this woman, and does their laundry. The man lives in an adjacent pocket of poverty.

Barbara (born in 1977), who is Hanna's daughter and Maria's granddaughter, also is a client of a social assistance office. She entered her adult life with almost no cultural, economic and social capital. Her father was an alcoholic. This is how she describes her childhood in her family home:

I *have only completed elementary school, I did not continue education because I had to repeat each year at school. It was very hard. Father beat me. He used to wake me up at midnight, he was drunk, and told me to sit at the table and study, to count and to read, and when I was stammering, he hit me on my head of course. And that was my life.*

The girl did not do well at school, she kept repeating years, and changed schools. Her future was predetermined already in the first year, when she had to be transferred to another school for the first time. That happened in the following circumstances: *I had to change schools very often, I asked the teacher, I raised my hand because I wanted to pee but she did not let me go out, she said that I could go for a pee during the break, and I could not wait any longer and peed, that happened in my first year and that is why I had to change schools. The teacher was laughing at me, so were the children.* Family roars and beating have lead to the following situation: *I kept having nightmares until I was 17 years old. I was waking up at night in tears. I also wetted my bed until I was 13 years old, I simply did not feel it. When I woke up, I stayed in the wet bedding and was afraid to get up and get beating from my father. I kept wetting myself all the time, I do not know whether it was fear or something else.* Barbara was isolated from children as she was an 'inappropriate' playmate. She reports: *As a matter of fact I had no friends. It is obvious that if a girl does not learn and receives 'C' at school, people look at her differently. I could have a girlfriend, but someone who would be the same as me, someone who did not learn, I did not learn, and the girls who were rich and received good grades, were another story.*

She completed elementary school only thanks to her grandmother, who took Barbara to her apartment and raised her for three years together with the grandson, Maria's foster son. Barbara resents her parents as they did not keep an eye on her to ensure that she went to school and did her homework. She was going to bed late at night as she was worried about her mum *that dad could hurt mum. He used to beat me – I was going to bed late at night as I was worried about my mum, that dad could hurt mum. Mum gave me away to grandma. I moved to grandma's when I was in the third year, and lived there until the fifth or sixth year. Grandma raised me there, I was going to school properly, I was doing homework after school, and then I could go out, the discipline at grandma's was completely different, an uncle, my mum's younger brother, also lived there, and he helped me with schoolwork. I passed from one year to another under his care. I visited mum at weekends.*

The girl completed elementary school with a delay, then got pregnant and got married very soon. Her mother-in-law bought a wedding dress for Barbara, and parents-in-law paid all cost of the wedding. *Mother-in-law bought me a wedding dress, as I was pregnant, the wedding reception was held at home, everything was held on the same day.* She reports: *I wanted to have a family and home very much, I wanted to separate from mum as soon as possible, I simply wanted to be my own boss, that is what I wanted. I chose a husband for myself. Initially, everything was beautiful and nice, he had money and a job, he was buying clothes for me, I thought that he would simply be wonderful. And now I have nothing. I would like to tell young girls not to rush into marriage and children.* The young couple moved into Barbara's father-in-law's apartment located in another poverty pocket. It is not clear whether the father-in-law lives with them or whether he left the apartment for them. The young couple has to pay rent and electricity bills. There are no other amenities available in this apartment. Currently Barbara's husband is unemployed. A child allowance provided by the social assistance is the only income available to this family. Grandmother and mother, who *give money to buy nappies for the child,* sporadically help them. In Barbara's opinion, the mother-in-law maintains the family, and maybe this is the reason why the son does not feel responsible for maintaining them. Barbara's husband leaves home every day at ten in the morning to search for a job, and is back at seven in the evening. *And there is no work, of course* – Barbara comments. *This is his daily ritual, and what can I do, what can I do?* Barbara had a temporary job as a seamstress assistant. She did not like the job *as I was a servant there... a doormat, she* [the boss] *could do whatever she liked.* She bought shoes for the child for the money she had earned. She is of the opinion that family maintenance is the husband's responsibility and that he *should take care of us, as simple as that.* That is why she declares: *I told him that I was not going to invest in the apartment, and things like that, I mean I am going to buy food of course, but only for the child, shoes for the child, everything for the child. If he is unable to take care of us, he wanted to have a family so he should take care of his home and family.* Barbara's husband does not meet these expectations and their marriage is at risk. Also due to the fact that our narrator feels very lonely as her husband *leaves her on her own. Of course that I miss home* – she continues her story – *I would like to go back to mum's, live at mum's provided that this current situation* [marriage], *is over. I live with my child, I am happy that I have such a wonderful child. I very often go to my mum's and to grandma's. You have to keep in touch with your family, I should not stay at home on my own, there is still time for this.*

Conclusions

The book presents the knowledge on intra- and inter-generational transmission of poverty perceived as a multidimensional phenomenon after the collapse of socialism. Our aim was to get a better understanding of social consequences which were caused by the collapse of socialism in the Central and Eastern Europe, based on examples of poverty perpetuation in the city of Łódź in Poland.

The central figures in the book are poor women belonging to four subsequent generations. They live in disadvantaged city districts, referred to as enclaves of poverty. They deserved specific attention because female labour force was very substantial in Łódź. The city was founded in the 19th century as a textile industry centre and the same path was followed until the upheaval in 1990. Rapid deindustrialization started at the very onset of capitalist social order and converted thousands of working class members into dependants on social assistance. Most of them were women, in socialism referred to as 'vanguard of female working class'. However, the sample did not only include workers of former state-owned factories. We also traced life paths of their descendant females. Therefore, the generations of the women that shared their family life stories with us included: (1) women born at the turn of the 1920s, and 1930s referred to as 'grandmothers'; (2) born in the mid-1950s called 'mothers', (3) born at the turn of the 1970s and 1980s referred to as 'daughters', and (4) 'granddaughters', born in the first two years after the return of Poland to capitalism, i.e. in the years 1989 and 1990.

The life-course perspective was applied in the research, and analyses conducted under the research followed the following five principles:

1. time and place; 2. linked lives; 3. human agency; 4. timing, and 5. life-span development. (Giele, Elder 1998; Elder, Johnson, Crosnoe 2004; Verd, Lopez 2011). The analysis was based on the assumption that the story is a means to access 'objective' reality beyond the narrator.

The specific objectives of analysing family life histories of women belonging to four subsequent generations were getting a better understanding of:

1) formative biographical events impacting women's entrenchment in poverty, its persistence and possible overcoming,
2) biographical experiences formative for each generation,
3) typical ways of experiencing biographical events by each generation,
4) socio-economic and historical processes underlying the course of subjective women's experiences,
5) patterns of experiencing poverty identified in all generations,
6) drivers and maintainers of poverty transmission across generations.

Focusing on women's life stories, we analysed them in the following biographical sequence: childhood, adolescence, adulthood and old age. We traced similarities and differences in the factors pushing members of the particular generations into poverty in specific life phases as well as in coping with hardship.

Socio-economic processes and social norms regarding the intimate relations differentiated opportunities and barriers for women belonging to subsequent generations. Structural factors and women' agency formed a frame for the poor living standard or pushed the narrators to temporary or persistent poverty.

Women belonging to the 'grandmothers' generation suffered from severe material deprivation during their childhood. The childhood and adolescence occurred in very traumatic periods of the Polish history: the inter-war period, the Second World War and the Nazi-German occupation. As children, the oldest interviewees were living in villages, often in reconstructed multi-children families of farmhands composed of step-father or step-mother and their children from previous marriages. Extreme poverty and malnutrition were their everyday experience. They worked to earn money and were overburdened with caring for younger siblings. Family migration to Łódź did not significantly improve their living conditions – newcomers occupied substandard housing and in the times of frequent lay-offs they had to live on social benefits. For those children and adolescents the WWII was the time of fear, hunger, forced displacement, forced labour in factories and farms in Germany. Nevertheless, this challenging, and in some cases, traumatic childhood equipped the eldest generation of women with a sense of agency, resourcefulness and ability to cope with difficulties.

The 'grandmothers' entered adulthood at the time of radical post-war political and economic changes (accelerated industrialisation, industry nationalisation) and social transformation (overcoming of illiteracy, health care provision for pregnant women and all children, education for free, a rise in women employment, paid maternity leave, etc.). Access to paid work (which did not avoid the job segmentation and segregation) accompanied by low wages, the patriarchal role model in a workplace and the family were the key factors that determined the opportunities and living conditions of the oldest generation of women. However, it was the first generation of female industrial workers in Poland history which could feel to be financially independent persons and when retired provided with an old-age pension.

While the post-war transformation was a chance for young people from families with a low social status, the next transformation (1989-2004) and the implementation of market economy reduced employment and lowered the standard of living among those of their descendants who were unable to use the opportunities offered by the socialist welfare state, by the educational policy in particular. The reason for missed opportunity to get a good education was often family relations during childhood and adolescence and the lack of social intervention provided on time. Many of respondents from the middle generation (aged 45-55 at the time of the research), found themselves in a group of people redundant in the market economy. To survive, they had to look for temporary work and relied on low social benefits and financial aids.

Material deprivation in the childhood of young and the youngest female respondents resulted from parents' inability to find a stable job and family relations, which led to child neglecting. They did not experience the system upheaval per se as an important biographical event. The world without a steady and secure job and 'living on welfare' seemed to be a 'normal' everyday situation. As adults, they accepted relying upon parents', or more frequently, on grandmothers' support and were less involved in searching for work. When they became single mothers, they considered social assistance benefits and child allowance as a 'normal', although insufficient, source of income.

Early school leaving is a formative experience of childhood and adolescence shared by poor women from all the generations. The 'grandmothers' did not complete primary school; vocational training was the maximum level of education the interviewed 'mothers' reached; 'daughters' graduated from an 8-grade primary school and 'granddaughters' from a 6-grade primary school. Members of the oldest generation had different reasons that contributed to this situation than respondents from the other age-groups. In the case of the eldest narrators, they were forced to interrupt their education due to historical events, such as Nazi-German occupation, and consequently forced labour. When Poland regained sovereignty, they felt too 'mature' to sit in a classroom, and had to work to support themselves and their relatives. Upon completion of vocational training in a factory, they obtained necessary skills to work there. People growing up after the WWII were provided with education for free, however 'mothers', 'daughters' and 'granddaughters' missed the opportunity.

In 'mothers' generation both parents were employed, but they suffered material deprivation due to low wages and alcohol abuse of the fathers. They desired to become independent of their parents, earn a living, and start a new life on their own. A large supply of vacancies in factories and other plants (later referred to as 'workers' labour market' made the process of hiring new staff easy. Some workers received vocational training, while others worked as low qualified staff members. Many members of this generation also became pregnant as teenagers, which led to discontinuation of education.

Women from the young and the youngest generations also shared the educational failure as the formative adolescence experience. 'Daughters' completed primary school late and with difficulties. Sometimes they learnt at schools for pupils with special educational needs. They grew up in families affected by unemployment, suffered from stress produced by material shortages and reconstruction of family relations when the divorced mother remarried. Step-fathers rejected them and behaved aggressively. They often were addicted to alcohol, just like their biological fathers. Grandmothers did not have much to offer but provided the girls with emotional and material support. Unfortunately they failed to awake their educational aspirations.

In 'granddaughters' generation, negative neighbourhood effects were recognised as playing truant, hanging out with *those guys*, and taking up risky behaviours. That often led to teenage motherhood. However, we noticed a difference between members of two young generations in terms of their approach to teenage motherhood. 'Daughters'' pregnancy was reported as accidental and unplanned, whereas the case of early motherhood of 'granddaughters' seems to be a deliberately chosen life strategy. Contrary to 'grandmothers' and 'mothers', for whom unplanned pregnancy was always a reason to marry the baby's father, 'daughters' and 'granddaughters' did not perceive marriage necessary. Representatives of the youngest generation decided to remain single as fathers of their children were alcohol and drug abusers, did not have jobs, were involved in criminal activities and sometimes were in prison. Fathers were also missing as they lived in a different location, were busy doing business or already started new relationships. Reactions toward teenage motherhood reflect an essential change in culture. Forced marriages due to teenage pregnancy have not been observed in the generations growing up at the turn of the 20th and the 21st century.

One can also observe substantial differences in adulthood-related behaviours. In biographical experience of the oldest generation of women, this phase first included taking up employment and only then getting married. Representatives of the 'grandmothers' generation usually worked all their lives in one factory, until retirement. Their marriages were also for life, even if husbands were irresponsible and caused problems.

Women of the 'mothers' generation began their adulthood with marriage (often a shotgun one – extorted by parents due to unplanned pregnancy) and took up employment later on. They got divorced, if not satisfied with a husband, and remarried when they met a new partner. It was also easy for them to change work until they became redundant on the labour market in the 1990s.

For women of 'daughters' and 'granddaughters' generations 'adulthood' is neither related to employment nor to marriage. 'Daughters' and 'granddaughters' either never performed any paid work, or tried to earn their living by taking up casual, unregistered jobs for very short periods of time. This second option characterised only a small group of respondents.

Therefore, subsequent generations of women, in the phase of their adulthood were at different levels of their financial independence and applied to different persons or institutions for support. Women of the generation of 'grandmothers' from their early childhood used to take responsibility for themselves and their closest relatives, and for securing all the needs with their effort, even when it required very hard work. In each life-course stage, they took actions to make a family budget balance. They became poverty managers (Tarkowska 2005). Their descendants relied on them. They provided shelters and food for their daughters and granddaughters who were unable to satisfy their needs. The youngest generation of 'granddaughters' could not be supported by their grandmothers, who themselves as members of 'mothers' generation, lived on a very modest old-age pension, if any, or on social assistance benefits. The youngest women who were residents of poverty enclaves, became welfare dependant.

Poor women's biographies showed that family resources necessary to equip their members with abilities and skills necessary to function in capitalist society were gradually shrinking, generation by generation. It indicates that an increased public spending will also be required in future. Breaking this vicious circle of poverty poses a challenge for intensifying investment in children living in poverty. It is documented that early child care and education is much more profitable for society than providing adults with different kinds of social benefits.

References

Airio I., Moisio P., Niemelä M. (2004), *Intergenerational Transmission of Poverty in Finland in the 1990s,* Department of Social Policy, Series C: 13/2004, University of Turku, Finland, available at:ttp://vanha.soc.utu.fi/sospol/julkaisut/Airio_Moisio_Niemela_5_b_nettiversio.pdf (09.07.2015)

Andrzejewski A. (1973), *Polityka mieszkaniowa i jej aspekty społeczne*, [in:] Rajkiewicz A. (eds.), „Polityka społeczna", Warszawa: PWE.

Arai L. (2009), *Teenage Pregnancy. The Making and Unmaking of a Problem*, Bristol/Portland: The Policy Press.

Balcerzak-Paradowska B. (1985), *Kredyty dla młodych małżeństw*, Warszawa: IPiSS.

Barberi P. (2007), *Atypical Employment and Welfare Regimes*, EQUALSOC, "Policy Paper", Vol. 1.

Barnett W. S., Belfield C. R. (2006), *Early Childhood Development and Social Mobility,* "Future of Children", Vol. 16, No. 2: 73–98.

Becker G. (1991), *A Treatise on the Family*, Harvard University Press.

Becker G., Tomes N. (1986), *Human Capital and the Rise and Fall of Families,* "Journal of Labor Economics", No. 4(2): S1–S139.

Beisert M. (1994), *Rozwód jako wydarzenie krytyczne w cyklu rozwoju rodziny*, „Problemy Rodziny", No. 2: 41–45.

Beisert M. (1994a), *Strategie zmagania się z rozwodem i jego następstwami*, „Problemy Rodziny", No. 6: 14–17.

Beisert M. (1995), *Psychologiczna sytuacja kobiet rozwiedzionych*, [in:] Miluska J., Pakszys E. (eds.), *Humanistyka i płeć. Studia Kobiece z psychologii, filozofii i historii,* Poznań: Wydawnictwo Naukowe UAM.

Berthoud R., Robson K. (2001), *The Outcomes of Teenage Motherhood in Europe. Innocenti Working Paper,* No. 86, Florence: UNICEF Innocenti Research Centre.

Bertaux D. (1981), *From the Life History Approach to the Transformation of Sociological Practice,* [in:] Bertaux D. (eds.), *Biography and Society, The Life History Approach in the Social Scientes,* Beverly Hills, London: Sage Publications Inc.

Bertaux D. (1995), *Case Histories of Families as a Method in Poverty Research*, referat prezentowany na konferencji: The Social History of Poverty in Europe, Budapeszt.

Beskid L. (1989), *Ekonomiczny i społeczny wymiar przemian warunków życia w latach 1980–85*, [in:] Beskid L. (eds.), *Warunki i sposób życia – zachowania przystosowawcze w kryzysie,* Warszawa: IFiS PAN.

Blanden J., Gibbons S. (2006), *The Persistence of Poverty Across Generations*, Bristol: The Policy Press, availableat: http://www.jrf.org.uk/bookshop/eBooks/9781861348531.pdf (06.04.2015).
Bojanowski T. (1992), *Łódź pod okupacja niemiecką w latach II wojny światowej (1939–1945)*, Łódź: Wydawnictwo UŁ.
Bojar H. (1991), *Rodzina i życie rodzinne,* [in:] Marody M. (eds.), *Co nam zostało z tych lat. Społeczeństwo polskie u progu zmiany systemowej*, Londyn: Aneks.
Bourdieu P., Passeron J.-C. (2006), *Reprodukcja. Elementy teorii systemu nauczania*, Warszawa: PWN.
Buck N. (2001), *Identifying Neighbourhood Effects on Social Exclusion*, "Urban Studies", No. 38, pp. 2251–2275.
Buck N., Gordon I. (2004), *Does spatial concentration of disadvantage contribute to social cohesion?,* [in:] Boddy M., Parkinson M. (eds.), *City Matters: Competitiveness, Cohesion and Urban Governance*, pp. 237–253. Bristol: Policy Press.
Chase-Lansdale P.L., Kiernan K., Friedman R. (eds.) (2004), *Human Development Across Lives and Generations*, Cambridge University Press, Cambridge.
Cichocki R. (1993), *Dane autobiograficzne a problem empiryczności,* [in:] Rzepa T., Leoński J. (eds.), *O Biografii i metodzie biograficznej*, Poznań: Wyd. Nakom.
Corcoran M., Adams T. (1997), *Race, Sex, and the Intergenerational Transmission of Poverty*, [in:] Duncan G. J., Brooks-Gunn J. (eds.), *Consequences of Growing Up Poor*, New York: Russell Sage Foundation.
Corcoran M. (2001), *Mobility, Persistence, and the Consequences for Children: child and Adult Outcomes*, [in:] Danziger S., Haveman R. (eds.) *Understanding Poverty*, Cambridge MA: Harvard University Press.
Daly M., Leonard M. (2002), *Against all Odds: Family Life on a Low Income in Ireland,* Dublin: Combat Poverty Agency/Institute of Public Administration.
De Neubourg C., Bradshaw J., Chzhen Y., Main G., Martorano B., Menchini L. (2012), *Child Deprivation, Multidimensional Poverty and Monetary Poverty in Europe,* Innocenti Working Paper, IWP-2012-02.
Denzin N. K. (1990), *Reinterpretacja metody biograficznej w socjologii: znaczenie a metoda w analizie biograficznej*, [in:] Włodarek J., Ziółkowski M. (eds.), *Metoda biograficzna w socjologii,* Warszawa: PWN.
Denzin N.K. (1989), *Interpretive Biography*, Sage Publication, London.
Dobrowolska D. (1992), *Przebieg życia, fazy, wydarzenia*, „Kultura i Społeczeństwo", No. 2: 75–87.
Dobrzyńska-Mesterhazy A. (1996), *Przemoc w rodzinie: diagnoza i interwencja kryzysowa,* [in:] Badura-Madej W. (eds.), Wybrane zagadnienia interwencji kryzysowej, Warszawa: Interart.
Elder Glen H., Kirkpatrick Johnson M., Crosnoe R. (2004), *The Emergence and Development of the Life Course Theory*, [in:] Mortimer J. T., Shanahan M. J. (eds.), *Handbook of the Life Course*, New York: Springer: 3–19.
Ellis-Sloan K. (2012), *'Becoming a Teenage Mother in the UK'*, PhD thesis, University of Brighton, Wielka Brytania.
Erdmans M.P., Black T. (2015), *On becoming a teen mom. Life before pregnancy*, Oakland: University of California Press.
Esping-Andersen G. (2004), *Children in the Welfare State. A Social Investment Approach,* http://www.recercat.net/bitstream/2072/2045/1/DEMOSOC10.pdf (1.10.2007).
Ermisch J. E. (2003), *Does a "Teen-birth" Have Longer-term Impacts on the Mother? Suggestive Evidence from the British Household Panel Study*, Working Papers of the Institute for Social and Economic Research, paper 2003 32, University of Essex, Colchester.

Garbarino J., Sherman D. (1980), *High Risks Neighborhoods and High-Risk Families: The Human Ecology of Child Maltreatment,* "Child Development", Vol. 51: 188–198.

Garmezy N., Rutter M. (1983), *Stress. Coping and Development in Children,* New York: McGraw-Hill.

Giele Janet Z., Elder Glen H. (1998), *The Life Course Mode of Inquiry,* [in:] Giele Janet Z., Elder Glen H. (eds.), *Methods of life course research. Qualitative and quantitative approaches,* Thousand Oaks, CA: Sage: 1–4.

Glaser B.G., Strauss A.L. (1968), *Time for Dying,* Aldine Publishing Com., Chicago.

Glaser B.G., Strauss A.L. (1970), *Anguish. A Case-History of a Dying Trajectory*, Sociology Press, California.

Goffman E. (1978), *Asylums. Essays on the Social Situation of Mental Patients and Other Inmates*, Penguin Books, Harmondsworth (ed. I 1961).

Goffman E. (1979), *Stigma. Notes in the Management of Spoiled Identity,* Penguin Books, Harmondsworth (ed. I 1961).

Golczyńska-Grondas A. (2004), *Mężczyźni z enklaw biedy. Rekonstrukcja pełnionych ról społecznych*, Łódź : Absolwent.

Golinowska S., Morecka Z., Styrc M., Cukrowska E., Cukrowski J. (2008), *Od ubóstwa do wykluczenia społecznego. Badania. Koncepcja. Wyniki. Propozycje. Polska, Europa i świat*, Warszawa: IPiSS.

Graham H., McDermott E. (2006), *Qualitative Research and the Evidence Base of Policy: Insights from Studies of Teenage Mothers in the UK*, "Journal of Social Policy", No. 35: 21–37.

Grotowska-Leder J. (2004), *Wielkomiejska bieda. Od epizodu do underclass.* Łódź: Wydawnictwo UŁ.

Growing Unequal. Income Distribution and Poverty in OECD Countries. (2008)

Hajduk E. (2001), *Kulturowe wyznaczniki biegu życia*, Warszawa: Wydawnictwo Akademickie „Żak".

Hankiss A. (1981), *Ontologies of the Self. On the Mythological Rearranging of One's Live History,* [in:] Bertaux D. (eds.), *Biography and Society, The Life History Approach in the Social Scientes,* Beverly Hills, London: Sage Publications Inc.

Harris Ch. (1987), *The Individual an Society: A Processual Approach,* [in:] Bryman A., Bytheway B., Allatt P., Keil T. (eds.), *Rethinking the Life Cykle,* British Sociological Association, London: 21–22.

Hoerning E. (1990), *Rola wydarzeń życiowych: doświadczenia i rewitalizacja w perspektywie biograficznej,* [in:] Włodarek J., Ziółkowski M. (eds.), *Metoda biograficzna w socjologii,* Warszawa: PWN.

Hrebenda A. (1996), *Życie codzienne bezrobotnych na Górnym Śląsku w okresie międzywojennym,* [in:] Borkowski T., Marcinkowski A. (eds.), *Socjologia bezrobocia,* Warszawa: Interart.

Imamura M., Tucker J., Hannaford P., Astin M., Oliveira da Silva M., Bloemenkap K.W.M., Karro H., Olsen J., Temmerman M. on behalf of the REPROSTAT 2 group (2006), *REPROSTAT2: A Systematic Review of Factors Associated with Teenage Pregnancy in the European Union. Final Report*, University of Aberdeen.

Jankowski B., Warzywoda-Kruszyńska W. (2013), *Ciągłość i zmiana w łódzkich enklawach biedy,* Łódź: Wydawnictwo Uniwersytetu Łódzkiego.

Jarosz M. (eds.) (2005), *Wygrani i przegrani polskiej transformacji*, Warszawa: Instytut Studiów Politycznych PAN.

Jażdżyńska J. (1958), *Kartki z życia łódzkiej kobiety,* Łódź: Łódzki Komitet Frontu Narodowego.

Jenkings S., Siedler T. (2007), *The Intergenerational Transmission of Poverty in Industrialized Countries,* CPRC Working Paper 77, Essex: Institute for Social and Economic Research University of Essex.

Johnson R. C. (2006), *Landing a Job in Urban Space: The Extent and Effects of Spatial Mismatch*, "Regional Science and Urban Economics", No. 36: 331–372.

Jundziłł I. (1993), *Dziecko – ofiara przemocy*, Warszawa: Wydawnictwa Szkolne i Pedagogiczne.

Kain J. F. (1968), *Housing Segregation, Negro Employment and Metropolitan Decentralization*, "Quarterly Journal of Economics", No. 82, pp.175–197.

Kohli M. (1981), *Biography: Account, Text, Method,* [in:] Bertaux D. (eds.), *Biography and Society. The Life History Approach in the Social Scientes,* Beverly Hills, London: Sage Publications Inc.

Korzeniewska K. (2002), *Biedni (i) emeryci: o ekonomicznej zależności biednych rodzin od pomocy społecznej z zewnątrz i o 'underclass po polsku',* [in:] Korzeniewska K., Tarkowska E. (eds.), *Lata tłuste, lata chude, spojrzenia na biedę w społecznościach lokalnych,* Warszawa: IFiS PAN.

Krzyszkowski J. (2005), *Między państwem opiekuńczym a opiekuńczym społeczeństwem*, Łódź: Wydawnictwo UŁ.

Landau Z., Tomaszewski J. (1981), *Zarys historii gospodarczej Polski 1918–1939*, Warszawa: Książka i Wiedza.

Leoński J. (1993), *Różne sposoby ujmowania metody biograficznej w socjologii*, [in:] Rzepa T., Leoński J. (eds.), *O Biografii i metodzie biograficznej,* Poznań: Nakom.

Lister R. (eds.) (1996), *Charles Murray and the Underclass. The Developing Debate,* London: Institute for Economic Affairs.

Ludwig J., Mayer S. (2006), *'Culture' and the Intergenerational Transmission of Poverty: the Prevention Paradox.* Future of children. Vol 16, No. 2: 175–196.

Marczyńska-Witczak E. (1996), *Zmiany struktury gospodarczej Łodzi,* [in:] Michalski W. (eds.), *Transformacja społeczno-gospodarcza Łodzi na tle regionu,* Łódź: Polskie Towarzystwo Geograficzne.

Marody M. (1991), *Jednostka w systemie realnego socjalizmu* [in:] Marody M. (eds.), *Co nam zostało z tych lat...*, Londyn: Aneks.

Marshall G. (2004), *Słownik Socjologii i Nauk społecznych*, Warszawa: PWN.

McCord C., Freeman H. P. (1990), *Excess Mortality in Harlem,* New England Journal of Medicine, Vol. 322: 173–177.

McMurrer D. P, Condon M., Sawhill I. V. (1997), *Intergenerational Mobility in the United States*, Companion Piece to Number 4 in Series, Opportunity in America, http://www.urban.org/publications/406796.html (1 of 23) (14.07. 2007).

Mead L. (1992), *The New Politics of Poverty: the Nonworking poor in America*, New York: Basic Books.

Miller R. (2007), *Using Family Histories to Understand the Intergenerational Transmission of Chronic Poverty. Chronic Poverty Research Centre*: Working Paper 103.

Minkowska A. (1996), *Rodzina bezrobotna*, [in:] Borkowski T., Marcinkowski A. (eds.), *Socjologia bezrobocia*, Warszawa: Interart.

Moore K. (2001), *Frameworks for Understanding the Intergenerational Transmission of Poverty and Well-being in Developing Countries*, CPRC Working Paper 8, *Chronic Poverty, International Development Department School of Public Policy*, University of Birmingham, http://www.chronicpoverty.org/resources/working_papers.html (17.05.2016)

Moore K. (2004), *Chronic, life-course and intergenerational poverty, and South-East Asian youth,* CPRC and Institute for Development Policy and Management (IDPM), School of Environment and Development, University of Manchester, United Kingdom, http://www.chronicpoverty.org/resources/working_papers.html (17.05.2016)

Munck Gerardo L. (2004), *Tools for Qualitative Research,* [in:] Brady H. E., Collier D. (eds.), *Rethinking social inquiry. Diverse tools, shared standards* (pp. 105–121), Lanham: Rowman and Littlefield.

Murray Ch. (1990), *The Emerging British Underclass*, London: Institute for Economic Affairs.

Music J.S, (1993), *Young, Poor and Pregnant. The Psychology of Teenage Motherhood*, Yale University.

Naugarten B.L., Hagestad G.O (1976), *Age and the Life Course,* [in:] Binstock R.H., Shanas E. (eds.), *Handbook of Aging and Social Sciences*, New York: Van Nostrand Reinhold.

O'Regan K., Wiseman M. (1989), *Brith Weights and the Geography of Poverty*, "Focus", Vol. 12: 16–22.

Osińska K., Śliwińska A. (1999), *Społeczności permanentnego ubóstwa: tożsamość kulturowa oraz percepcja kultury polskiej i stratyfikacji społecznej,* [in:] Mucha J. (eds.), Kultura dominująca jako kultura obca, Warszawa: Oficyna Naukowa.

Palska H. (1999), *Zależeć od innych. Formy aktywności ekonomicznej ludzi ubogich*, „Polityka Społeczna", No. 11/12: 6–9.

Palska H. (2000), *Czy nowe style życia Polaków. Wybrane wymiary stylu życia 'ludzi sukcesu'*, [in:] Domański H., Ostrowska A., Rychard A. (eds.), *Jak żyją Polacy*, Warszawa: IFiS PAN.

Perepeczko B. (2002), *Swoistość biedy w rodzinach rolniczych i jej oswajanie,* [in:] Tarkowska E. (eds.), *Przeciw biedzie*, Warszawa: Oficyna Naukowa.

Piketty T. (2000), *Theories of Persistent Inequality and Intergenerational Mobility*, [in:] Atkinson A. B., Bourguignon F. (eds.), *Handbook of Income Distribution,* Amsterdam: North Holland.

Pospiszyl I. (1994), *Przemoc w rodzinie*, Warszawa: Wydawnictwa Szkolne i Pedagogiczne.

Potoczna M., Warzywoda-Kruszyńska W. (2009), *Kobiety z łódzkich enklaw biedy. Bieda w cyklu życia i międzypokoleniowym przekazie*, Łódź: Wydawnictwo Uniwersytetu Łódzkiego.

Prawda M. (1989), *Biograficzne odtwarzanie rzeczywistości,* „Studia Socjologiczne", No. 4.

Przemoc w Rodzinie wobec kobiet i dzieci (2000), Warszawa: Fundacja Centrum Praw Kobiet.

Przetacznik-Gierowska M., Tyszkowa M. (1996), *Psychologia rozwoju człowieka. Zagadnienia ogólne*, Warszawa: PWN.

Rokuszewska-Pawełek A. (1996), *Doświadczenia wojenne Polaków – analiza trajektorii wrześniowej*, [in:] Czyżewski A., Piotrowski A., Rokuszewska-Pawełek A. (eds.), *Biografia a tożsamość narodowa*, Łódź: Wydawnictwo UŁ.

Rutter M. (1994), *Continuities, Transitions and Turning Points in Development,* [in:] Rutter A., Hay D. F. (eds.), *Development Throuhg Life: A Handbook for Clinicians,* Oxford: Blackwell Scientific Publications.

Rutter M. (1987), *Psychosocial resilience and protective mechanisms*, "American Journal of Orthopsychiatry", No. 57(3): 316–330.

Sampson R. J. (2009), *Disparity and Diversity in the Contemporary City: Social (Dis)order Revisited,* "British Journal of Sociology", Vol. 60, Issue 1: 1–31, http://www3.interscience.wiley.com/cgi-bin/fulltext/122261218/PDFSTART (19.09.2016).

Smykowski J. (2002), *Parobek. Historia społeczna ziem Królestwa Polskiego na przełomie wieków XIX i XX jako historia ubóstwa,* [in:] Korzeniewska K., Tarkowska E. (eds.), *Lata tłuste, lata chude, spojrzenia na biedę w społecznościach lokalnych*, Warszawa: IFiS PAN.

Sztander W. (1995), *Rodzina z problemem alkoholowym*, Warszawa: Instytut Psychologii Zdrowia i Trzeźwości.
Szukalski P. (2004), *Kohabitacje w Polsce. Separacje w Polsce. Bezdzietność w Polsce. Urodzenia pozamałżeńskie w Polsce*, [in:] Warzywoda-Kruszyńska W., Szukalski P. (eds.), *Rodzina w zmieniającym się społeczeństwie polskim*, Łódź: Wydawnictwo UŁ.
Schutze F. (1981), *Prozessstrukturen des Lebensabkaufs,* [in:] Mathes J., et al. *Biographie der handkungswissenschaftlicher Perspektive*, Verlag der Nurnberger Forschungsvereinigung, Nurnberg: 67–156.
Schutze F. (1983), *Bioggraphieforschung und narratives Interview,* Neue praxix, No. 3: 283–293.
Sharkey P. T., Tirado-Strayer N., Papachristos A.V., Raver C. C. (2012), *The Effect of Local Violence on Children's Attention and Impulse Control*, "American Journal of Public Health", No. 102(12), 2287–2293.
Shildrick T., McDonald R., Webster C., Garthwaite K. (2012), *Poverty and Insecurity. Life in Low-pay, No-pay Britain,* Bristol: The Policy Press, University of Bristol.
Shonkoff J.P., Philips D. A. (eds.), (2000), *From Neurons to Neighborhoods. The Science of Early Childhood Development,* National Academy Press, Washington D.C.
Shanahan M. J., Mortimer J. T., Krikpatrick Johnson M. (eds.) (2016), *Handbook of the Life Cours*, Vol. II, Springer International Publishing Switzerland.
Shonkoff J.P. (2011), *Building on Foundations for Prosperity on the Science of the Early Child Development*, "Pathways. A Magazine on Poverty, Inequality and Social Policy", Winter: 10–16.
TARKI Social Research Institute and Applica (2010), *Child poverty and child wellbeing in the European Union,* Report prepared for the DG Employment, Social Affairs and Equal Opportunities (Unite E.2) of the European Commission, Budapest.
Tarkowska E. (2000), *Zróżnicowanie biedy: wiek i płeć,* [in:] Domański H., Ostrowska A., Rychard A. (eds.), *Jak żyją Polacy,* Warszawa: IFiS PAN.
Tarkowska E., Warzywoda-Kruszyńska W., Wódz K. (2003), *Biedni o sobie i swoim życiu*, Katowice: Wydawnictwo Śląsk.
Teenage Pregnancy Independent Advisory Group (2008), *Annual Report 2007/08*, London: Department for Children, Schools and Families.
UNICEF (2001), *A League Table of Teenage Births in Rich Nations*, "Innocenti Report Card", No.3, Innocenti Research Centre, Florencja.
UNICEF (2013), *Dzieci w Polsce. Dane, liczby, statystyki*, Warszawa: Polski Komitet Narodowy UNICEF.
Verd J. M., Lopez M. (2011), *The Rewards of a Qualitative Approach to Life-Course Research. The Example of the Effects of Social Protection Policies on Career Paths*, "Forum Qualitative Social Research", Vol. 12, No. 3, Art. 15
Wacquant L. (2008), *Ghettos and Anti-Ghettos: An Anatomy of the New Urban Poverty, Thesis Eleven* 94 (August 2008): 113–118, http://sociology.berkeley.edu/faculty/wacquant/wacquant_pdf/GHETTOSANTIGHETTOS pub.pdf (14.04.2016).
Wacquant L. (2009), *Więzienia nędzy,* Warszawa: Instytut Wydawniczy Książka i Prasa.
Wacquant L. (2007), *Territorial Stigmatization in the Age of Advanced Marginality*, *Thesis Eleven* 91 (November 2007): 66–77.
Wacquant L. (2008), *Urban Outcasts*. Malden: The Polity Press.
Walczak R. (2000), *Obraz siebie u kobiet długotrwale bezrobotnych*, Lublin: KUL.
Warzywoda-Kruszyńska W. (eds.) (2001), *Lokalne strategie przeciwdziałania bezrobociu i biedzie*, Łódź: Instytut Socjologii UŁ.
Warzywoda-Kruszyńska W. (2003), *Samorządy lokalne wobec bezrobocia i biedy*, Łódź: Instytut Socjologii UŁ.

Warzywoda-Kruszyńska W. (2003a), *„Oswajanie" biedy w trzech pokoleniach Łodzian*, [in:] Doktór K., Konecki K., Warzywoda-Kruszyńska W. (eds.) *Polska, gospodarka, społeczeństwo*, Łódź: Wydawnictwo UŁ.

Warzywoda-Kruszyńska W., Krzyszkowski J. (1990), *Młode małżeństwa w wielkim mieście*, Łódź: Instytut Socjologii UŁ.

Warzywoda-Kruszyńska W. (eds.) (1998, 2001), *Żyć i pracować w enklawach biedy*, Łódź: Instytut Socjologii UŁ.

Warzywoda-Kruszyńska W. (eds.) (1999, 2001), *(Żyć) Na marginesie wielkiego miasta*, Łódź: Instytut Socjologii UŁ.

Warzywoda-Kruszyńska W. (eds.) (2001), *Lokalne strategie przeciwdziałania biedzie i bezrobociu?*, Łódź: Instytut Socjologii UŁ.

Warzywoda-Kruszyńska W., Grotowska-Leder J., Krzyszkowski J. (2003), *Lokalna polityka wobec biedy i pomocy społecznej*, Łódź: Instytut Socjologii UŁ.

Warzywoda-Kruszyńska W., Grotowska-Leder J. (1996), *Wielkomiejska bieda. Klienci pomocy społecznej w okresie transformacji*, Łódź: Instytut Socjologii UŁ.

Warzywoda-Kruszyńska W., Grotowska-Leder J., Krzyszkowski J. (2003), *Lokalna polityka wobec biedy i pomocy społecznej*, Łódź: Instytut Socjologii UŁ.

Werner E. F., Smith E. S. (1982), *Vulnerable but Inevicible: a Longitudinal Study of Resilient Children and Youth,* New York: McGraw-Hill.

Wiggins M., Oakley A., Sawtell M., Austerberry H., Clemens F., Elbourne D. (2005), *Teenage Parenthood and Social Exclusion: a multi-method study. Summary report of findings,* London: Social Science Research Unit Report, Institute of Education.

Wilson W. J. (1987), *The Truly Disadvantaged: the Inner City, the Underclass and Public Policy*, Chicago: University of Chicago Press.

Yaqub S. (2000), *Intertemporal Welfare Dynamics. Background Paper for HDR*, http://hdr.undp.org/docs/publications/background_papers/yaqub.doc (22.07.2007).

Yaqub S. (2001), *Intertemporal Welfare Dynamics. Background Paper for HDR*, http://hdr.undp.org/docs/publications/background_papers/yaqub.doc (dostęp 11.07.2007).

Yaqub S. (2002), *Chronic Poverty: Scrutinizing Estimates, Patterns, Correlates, and Explanations*, Working Paper No 21, Poverty Research Unit, School of African and Asian Studies, Sussex University, Falmer, Brighton.

Yaqub S. (2002), "*Poor children grow into poor adults": harmful mechanisms or over-deterministic theory?* "Journal of International Development", No. 14: 1081–1093.

Założenia polityki mieszkaniowej (1994), Sprawy mieszkaniowe, nr 4.

http://sociology.berkeley.edu/faculty/wacquant/wacquant_pdf/TERRITORIALSTIGMATIZATION.pdf (12.10.2016).

About the authors

Paulina Bunio-Mroczek, PhD in sociology, assistant professor at the Department of Applied Sociology and Social Work at the Institute of Sociology of the University of Łódź. Her academic interests concentrate around the issues of poverty, social exclusion, social work and gender. She teaches at social work, sociology and social policy bachelor's and master's programs. She is also interested in social changes of postindustrial cities resulting from revitalization programs.

Małgorzata Potoczna, PhD in sociology, assistant professor at the Department of Applied Sociology and Social Work at the Institute of Sociology of the University of Łódź. The main area of her research interests is the issue of poverty and social exclusion, with a particular emphasis on the sociology of the life course and biographical experiences of people at risk of social marginalisation and social exclusion. Małgorzata Potoczna also focuses on social work teaching and social welfare changes in the context of active integration measures provided to the socially excluded. Her field of research is also evaluation of projects in social work and social workers education.

Wielisława Warzywoda-Kruszyńska, full professor of sociology at the University of Łódź. Director of the Institute of Sociology for 16 years, she also chaired the Department of General Sociology, and the Department of Applied Sociology and Social Work. She contributed to the establishment of a major in Social Work at the Institute of Sociology. From the very start of her scientific career, Prof. Warzywoda-Kruszyńska's research interests have been focused on the transformation of social structure in Poland as it is broadly understood, including the topics of poverty and social exclusion which she has persistently pursued since the early 1990s. One of the outcomes of several research projects conducted in this area is her thesis of *juvenalization of poverty in Poland*. Moreover, Prof. Warzywoda-Kruszyńska has participated in numerous international research projects, including the PROFIT project funded by the European Union as part of the 6th Framework Programme where she served as a coordinator. She is the author or co-author of 34 monographs and more than 120 scientific articles. Prof. Warzywoda-Kruszyńska is a winner of the programme 'Master of the Foundation for Polish Science'. She is a member of numerous Polish and international scientific associations.

REVIEWER
Danuta Duch-Krzystoszek

INITIATING EDITOR
Iwona Gos

CO-TRANSLATOR
Guy Cole

LINGUISTIC EDITOR
Donata Mathews

TYPESETTING
Munda – Maciej Torz

COVER DESIGN
Katarzyna Turkowska

COVER IMAGE
© Depositphotos.com/RomanNerud

Publication without the editorial review at the publishing house of the University of Łódź

First Edition. W.07717.16.0.K

Publisher's sheets 9.0; printing sheets 10.5